# BIG DOGS little DOGS

# BIG DOGS little DOGS

## the world of our canine companions

A Lookout Book

GT
PUBLISHING

Copyright © 1998 GT Publishing

Produced by Lookout
1024 Avenue of the Americas
New York, New York  10018

Picture credits are on page 188.

Endpaper photograph by Jason Walz.

A&E is a registered trademark of A&E Television Networks

Published in 1998 by GT Publishing Corporation
16 E. 40th Street
New York, New York  10016

Library of Congress Cataloging-in-Publication Data

Big dogs, little dogs: the world of our canine companions,
        p.   cm.
    "The companion volume to the A&E special presentation."
    "A Lookout book."
    ISBN 1-57719-353-9 (hardcover)
    1. Dogs.  2. Dogs—United States.    I. Arts and Entertainment
Network.
SF426.2.855  1998
636.7—dc21                                             98-23212

Printed in the United States of America

10  9  8  7  6  5  4  3  2  1

First Printing

# CONTENTS

# INTRODUCTION

---

This is a book about dogs—big dogs, little dogs, famous dogs, and not-so-famous dogs. Like all true dog books, it is also about what ASPCA president Roger Caras calls "that funny-looking, two-legged dog who runs the can opener."

Sometime in the distant past, most likely on a dark and stormy night, a deal was struck between humans and dogs. It was a landmark event, a turning point in human history. The exact terms of that ancient agreement are long forgotten, but they seem to include permission to rub dogs' stomachs, scratch behind their ears, talk to them, work with them, play with them, and, yes, weep for them when they die. In return we get licks and barks and wagging tails, and unbridled loyalty and affection. James Thurber, whose stories and drawings capture the essence of being canine, figured man and dog teamed up at the dawn of human history. "It did not take man long— probably not more than a hundred centuries—to discover that all the animals except the dog were impossible around the house," he wrote. "One has but to spend a few days with an aardvark or a llama, command a water buffalo to sit up and beg, or try to housebreak a moose, to perceive how wisely man set about his process of elimination and selection."

The Kato Indians of northern California placed the origins of the bond even earlier. According to Kato legend, the Great Traveler, the god Nagaicho, didn't create the dog when he made the Earth and the other animals; he already had one. For the Kato, it was unthinkable for a god not to have a dog. After Nagaicho made the Earth he traveled over it, creating humans, animals, rivers, and mountains as he

55 MILLION DOGS FEEL AT HOME IN 35 MILLION AMERICAN HOUSEHOLDS.

went along, proudly showing them to his dog. Another Kato myth tells how the coyote, cousin to the dog, created the moon and stars. It seems the sun, tied down and covered with a blanket, originally lived in a house. The coyote stole the sun when its guardians were sleeping and cut it up into a sun, moon, and stars. The coyote then told these new heavenly bodies when and where to appear in the sky and presented them to the Kato people.

Literature is full of stories about the creation of the dog. According to the poet Rainer Maria Rilke, "God sat down for a moment when the dog was finished in order to watch it . . . and to know that it was good, that nothing was lacking, that it could not have been made better." The jackal-headed Egyptian god Anubis, half human

and half canine, was an early step toward deifying our four-legged companions. In this century, Ambrose Bierce took it all the way, defining the dog as "a kind of additional or subsidiary Deity designed to catch the overflow and surplus of the world's worship." The Chinese assign every twelfth year in their zodiac to our canine partners. Harry Houdini, Shirley MacLaine, Judy Garland, Sylvester Stallone, Donald Sutherland, and Michael Jackson were all born in the Year of the Dog. The next one will be in 2006.

We have glorified dogs in other ways in the twentieth century. There was Rin Tin Tin and Lassie and Benji, and now a feisty Jack Russell terrier named Eddie, costar of the popular sitcom *Frasier*. And since October 4, 1950, there has been an extroverted, daydreaming beagle with a Walter Mitty complex known as Snoopy— a.k.a. Joe Cool, World War I Flying Ace, Literary Ace ("It was a dark and stormy night . . ."), Flashbeagle, and Foreign Legionnaire beagle. We buy things on the recommendation of dogs—"Dogs love trucks!"—and have even absorbed them into

DIRECT ANCESTOR OF THE DOG, THE WOLF IS A FIERCE HUNTER THAT CAN BRING DOWN PREY 10 TIMES ITS OWN WEIGHT.

our language. After all, in this dog-eat-dog world we too often get sick as a dog working like a dog to satisfy the top dog and stay out of the doghouse so that maybe, once in a while, we can put on the dog. That's official dogma.

But why have we raised the humble pooch to such lofty heights? What is it about dogs that makes us so crazy about them? Words like *loyalty*, *bravery*, and *unquestioning devotion* come to mind, but there's more to it than that. Dogs ground us. They bring us back to a simpler world, one without meetings and mortgages and the rest of the baggage of human society. In a dog's world the important things are food and walks and fooling around, and it's perfectly okay to take a nap any time you feel like it. Dogs keep us from taking ourselves too seriously. "The great pleasure of

a dog," wrote Samuel Butler, "is that you may make a fool of yourself with him and not only will he not scold you, but he will make a fool of himself too."

Clearly both sides in the deal between humans and dogs have flourished. Today in the United States there are 269 million of us and about 55 million of them. We spend upward of $18 billion annually to maintain the relationship and, for the most part, we

think it's worth it. Dogs not only give us companionship and love but also guard our property and our children, herd our livestock, rescue our lost and injured, and provide eyes for the blind, ears for the deaf, and comfort and assistance for the ill and infirm. Says Roger Caras: "It's rare that you find a dog owner that doesn't classify the dog as a member of the family. . . . People and dogs bond extremely well. . . . The dog's size makes it convenient; its skills retrieving, herding, hunting, guarding, and cuddling make it useful. The fact that it is a pack animal just as we are makes it amiable. And once you squeeze a puppy, well, it's all over. The deal is done."

The notion that the dog is man's best friend probably dates back to prehistoric

DOGS ARE INHERENTLY PLAYFUL, A VESTIGE OF PACK BEHAVIOR INHERITED FROM THE WOLVES.

times, but the man who first coined the phrase was a Missouri lawyer named George Graham Vest. In 1870 Vest, who later became a U.S. senator, argued the case for Charles Burden, a man whose beloved hunting dog Old Drum was shot to death by his neighbor. "The one absolute, unselfish friend that man can have in this selfish world—the one that never proves ungrateful or treacherous—is his dog," Vest told the jury in his celebrated summation. "Gentlemen of the jury, a man's dog stands by him in prosperity and poverty, in health and sickness. He will sleep on the cold ground, where the wintry winds blow, and the snow drives fiercely, if only he can be near his master's side. He will kiss the hand that has no food to offer; he will lick the wounds and sores that come in encounter with the roughness of the world." And the effusive Vent didn't stop there. "When the last scene of all comes, and death takes the master in its embrace, and his body is laid away in the cold ground, no matter if all other friends pursue their way, there by his graveside will the noble dog be found, his head between his paws, his eyes sad but open in alert watchfulness, faithful and true even to death." The jury, moved to tears, ruled in Vent's favor and his client was awarded $50 in damages. Today, thanks to Vent's impassioned speech, a statue of Old Drum stands on the Johnson County courthouse lawn in Warrensburg, Michigan, a tribute to noble dogs everywhere.

But so much for what *we* think about dogs. What do dogs think about us? The question itself raises another question: Do dogs, in fact, think? For much of recorded history, especially in Christian nations, the opinion of philosophers and scholars was a resounding *no*. Dogs were considered machines, bundles of preprogrammed instincts wrapped in a fur sack. They could not be intelligent or possess emotions because then they would have *souls*. Descartes himself championed this position in the seventeenth century, making it hard to believe he ever owned a dog; he certainly never watched his dog push a chair across a room and up to a table in order to climb up and steal food. Few philosophers today would dare claim that dogs don't think—but what do they think *about*? Novelist and Nobel laureate John Steinbeck thought he knew: "I've seen a look in dogs' eyes," he wrote, "a quickly vanishing look of amazed contempt, and I am convinced that basically dogs think humans are nuts."

THE DEAL WITH DOGS IS SEALED WITH A COOL DRINK.

# chapter one

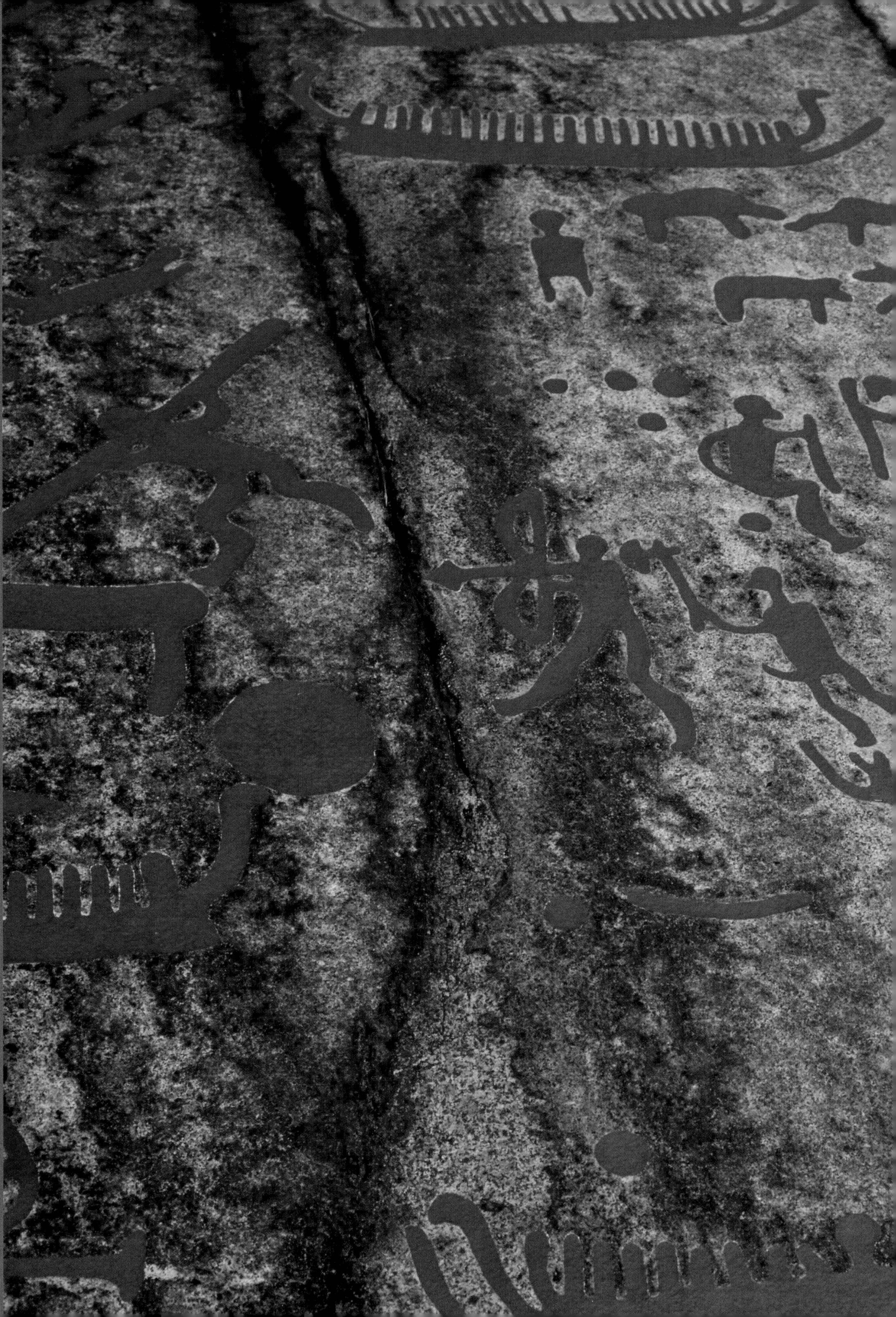

DOGS ASSIST IN THE HUNT IN THIS 3,000-YEAR-OLD BRONZE AGE PETROGLYPH.

# THE

According to the latest scientific evidence, the deal between humans and dogs was struck at least 14,000 years ago. That's the estimated age of the discovered fossil remains of a dog who lived with humans in a cave in what is now Iraq. In southern Europe archaeologists found the remains of a young Stone Age girl and four dogs in an excavated grave thought to be more than 10,000 years old. The dogs were strategically placed, each facing a different direction, perhaps to guard the girl in the afterlife. Similar Stone Age dwellings shared by dogs and humans have been found in China and the United States, suggesting that the dog at that time was already distributed over most of the world. In Switzerland and Denmark 10,000 years ago two distinct types of dogs had already emerged: one large and one small, presumably a work dog and a house dog.

Most scientists studying the evolution of the dog believe that man's best friend is a

# HISTORICAL

direct descendant of the wolf. Some say the dog is no more than a domesticated wolf, a wolf in sheep's clothing. Scientists cannot distinguish between a wolf and a dog from DNA analysis alone, but from studies of the genes of various breeds of dogs some biologists now believe the divergence of wolf and dog took place more than 100,000 years ago. If true, this finding raises an intriguing possibility: Our prehistoric ancestors, perhaps Neanderthals, may have kept dogs before we appeared on the scene.

How did it all begin? Perhaps some ancient human found a wolf puppy and brought it home for the clan's dinner. Puppies being what they are, if there were children around the camp, the rest is obvious. The clan must have settled for pizza that night. Or perhaps some prehistoric band of hunter-gatherers, sitting around the campfire, decided to throw scraps of food to the nearby wolves to stop them from howling. If the feeding continued, the wolves may have begun traveling

# DOG

FOR WOLVES, DOGS, AND HUMANS, FAMILY COMES FIRST.

with the human pack, eventually considering it their own. At some point the clan might have encountered other clans and presented them with a puppy or two as barter for food or simply as a gesture of friendship. Later on perhaps, the clans started interbreeding their domesticated wolves in hopes of producing animals even better suited to their lifestyle.

California dog trainer Sapir Weiss puts a different spin on the story: "Let's start from the beginning . . . who domesticated whom? Did humans domesticate wolves or wolves domesticate humans? I really believe that wolves domesticated humans. Without the wolf we would not be as far advanced as we are today. It would have taken us maybe another few thousand years to be where we are."

By the time humans first began recording their histories and adventures the dog was everywhere. Slim, elegant, greyhoundlike sight hounds, the ancestors of today's pharaoh, saluki, Ibizan, basenji, and Afghan hounds, were popular in ancient Egypt. In fact, ancient Egyptians of every rank kept dogs, ranging from large, ferocious guard dogs to small, short-legged, pot-bellied dogs that were beloved household companions. The actual names of some of these dogs—Blackie, Spot, Useless, and Cookpot, to name a few—are found inscribed on the walls of Egyptian tombs.

The ancient Greeks kept dogs and built the cult of the hunt around them. Some of these dogs were so admired that at banquets they ate at the table with the hunters and shared in the sacrifices to the gods of the hunt. Many ancient Greek burial sites contain elaborate inscriptions to the dogs owned by the deceased. The idea of the dog's unparalleled loyalty dates back at least to the Greeks: When Odysseus returned from his epic journey, only his faithful dog, Argus, recognized him.

The Romans treasured dogs for their loyalty and their ferocity, as did Atilla the Hun, who used giant Molossian dogs, precursors of the mastiff, and Talbots, ancestors of the bloodhound, in his campaigns. The Romans pitted Irish wolfhounds and mastiffs against human gladiators, lions, leopards, and even elephants in the Coliseum. The Romans also established a healing cult around dogs that lasted more than a thousand years. The cult operated temples stocked with sacred dogs. Says anthropologist and dog historian Mary Elizabeth Thurston: "If you had something

WOLF DIORAMA, SMITHSONIAN INSTITUTION, WASHINGTON, D.C., 1995.

that ailed you, you went in and saw a priest. He led you into a room full of dogs and you lay on the floor and let the dogs diagnose you by sniffing you and licking different body parts. People claimed miraculous cures by these dogs and the temples were filled with written testimonials about people being cured of blindness, all kinds of tumors." And at one Roman site near Pompeii, archaeologists unearthed the remains of a dog buried with a child. The dog wore a silver collar indicating that its name was Delta and that it belonged to Severinus, whose life the dog had saved from a wolf.

The ancient Chinese bred dogs for fighting (the shar-pei), hunting (the chow chow), and as a supplemental food supply. They also created one of the true canine masterpieces, the tiny Pekinese, as a royal pet. Bred exclusively for the Imperial Family, for over a thousand years the Pekinese was not seen outside the Forbidden City, where some were so pampered they had their own human servants. The penalty for stealing one was death. During the Opium Wars of the nineteenth century, French and British troops stormed the summer palace of the Dowager Empress and found a pack of Pekinese, and they became the first of their kind to travel from the Orient. One was presented to Queen Victoria, and soon Pekinese became the rage of Europe.

During the Middle Ages, purebred hounds were a status symbol of not only nobility but church officials as well, and many monasteries specialized in dog breeding. The most famous was the Abbey of St. Hubert at Mouzon, in the Ardennes region of France, where descendants of the favorite hounds of Saint Hubert, the seventh-century patron saint of dogs and the hunt, were bred. From St. Hubert Hounds came

today's bloodhounds, so called because they were purebred or "blooded" rather than "bloodthirsty." Around this time the notion of upper-class dogs (purebreds) and lower-class dogs (mongrels) began to take hold. In parts of Europe it became illegal to own certain purebred hunting dogs; if you did, you were presumed to be poaching on royal lands. The idea that dogs, like humans, are divided into bluebloods and peasants unfortunately persists today.

Of course, European peasants produced breeds to fit their own needs—terrierlike dogs to handle vermin, large dogs to pull carts, and short-legged, long-bodied dogs known as *turnspits*, designed to run on treadmills that powered such things as water wheels, butter churns, and roasting spits. The harsh treatment of cart dogs and turnspits became a central issue in the humane movement in Europe in the nineteenth century and was among the primary reasons that a U.S. diplomat named Henry Bergh founded the American Society for the Prevention of Cruelty to Animals in 1866.

Throughout history dogs have played the role of hero, showing bravery under fire, saving lives (often by sacrificing their own), and bringing comfort to the injured and infirm. One such hero was Stubby, a Connecticut mongrel thought to have been part Boston terrier and part boxer. At the beginning of World War I the New Haven campus of Yale University was being used as an army training base, and Stubby, a local stray, was adopted by the troops. When the soldiers shipped out to France they smuggled Stubby aboard and afterward were never sorry they did. Stubby took part in nineteen battles during his eighteen months at the front. He warned the troops of mustard gas attacks and snipers and reputedly even caught a German spy by the seat

of the pants—just as the spy was smuggling tactical maps and other documents out of camp. Twice he was wounded, which is how his true service came into play: He was sent to a hospital in Paris to recuperate and wound up becoming a therapy dog long before anyone had ever heard of therapy dogs. Stubby would hobble up and down the corridors, visiting soldiers in their beds and bringing a kind of comfort not offered by doctors and nurses.

When he returned to the United States Stubby's picture was plastered across the front page of newspapers throughout the country and he led more parades than any dog before or since. During his service, Stubby became the first animal ever promoted to sergeant in the U.S. Army. He was invited to the White House by President Woodrow Wilson and was awarded a gold medal by General Pershing. When Stubby died in 1926 his cremated remains were placed in a plaster replica of his body, which was then covered by his skin. This monument to one of America's true war heroes now resides at the Smithsonian in Washington, D.C.

The history of dogs is now and always has been inexorably linked to the history of man. When we go to war, they go to war. When we treat each other more humanely, we seem to treat them better as well. Dogs take the bad with the good. The patent-medicine shows of the nineteenth and early twentieth centuries not only sold snake oil for people but also a variety of 90-proof miracle concoctions touted to improve your dog's behavior or calm dogs in heat. And in the 1950s, when Americans decided that cooking was bothersome and boring and invented the fast-food culture we live in today, the concept of commercial dog food for our canine companions was born. "It's amazing that in just two generations we now have a population that can't remember ever feeding their dogs anything but canned dog food or bagged kibble," says Mary Elizabeth Thurston. "My father grew up on a ranch in Texas in the 1920s and used to watch his grandfather make dog bread from a recipe he had brought to this country from Wales. In the nineteenth century, the Welsh ground corn expressly for this corn bread they baked, poured milk over, and served to the ranch dogs. That's all the dogs ever ate. That and watermelon in the summertime. They had dogs that lived to be seventeen and eighteen years old."

DINGO DIORAMA, AMERICAN MUSEUM OF NATURAL HISTORY, NEW YORK, 1995.

What's next? Reports say that more and more of us, concerned about cholesterol and preservatives and other nasty ingredients, are starting to cook for our dogs again. There are even programs dedicated to canine cuisine on the Food Channel. History appears to be repeating itself. A few fearless futurists have speculated that dogs soon may be using computers, although the prevailing opinion among dog owners on the Internet seems to be that dogs don't like computers. Among the reasons given: dogs find it hard to look at a monitor with their head cocked to one side, dogs can't stick their heads out of Windows 95, and dogs are not geeks.

A COURAGEOUS FRENCH
CANINE (LEFT), READY
TO CARRY A MESSAGE
TO HIS COMRADES
DURING WORLD WAR I.
BRAVE AND LOYAL DOGS
(ABOVE, RIGHT) SERVED
IN THE NEXT WORLD
WAR AS WELL.

# the dog depicted

Early man painted images of dogs on the walls of caves in Spain some 12,000 years ago. Before that, Stone Age humans must have realized that if you fold your index finger and extend your thumb, the shadow cast in the firelight is the profile of a dog. Move your little finger and the shadow-dog barks.

Ancient Egyptians, Greeks, and Romans portrayed dogs in paintings, sculpture, and pottery, many of them resembling the greyhounds and mastiffs of today. Dogs are noticeably absent in early European Christian art, but return in full favor by the eleventh century, as depicted in numerous period tapestries. During the Renaissance, Titian, Velásquez, Van Eyck, and Dürer all painted dogs, and Leonardo da Vinci produced detailed anatomical studies. Since then the dog has captured the imagination of artists ranging from Thomas Gainsborough in the eighteenth century to Andy Warhol in the twentieth.

TUTANKHAMEN ON A CHARIOT AIMING HIS ARROW AT AN OSTRICH. FAN-SHAPED HEADPIECE FROM THE TOMB OF TUTANKHAMEN. GOLD, METAL, AND WOOD. 1350 B.C.E.

*THE DEATH OF ACTAEON.* RED-FIGURE POTTERY, 5TH–6TH CENTURY B.C.E.

*CAVE CANEM* (BEWARE THE DOG). ROMAN MOSAIC FROM THE THRESHOLD OF A HOUSE IN POMPEII. 1ST CENTURY B.C.E.

*TOBIAS AND SARAH.* STAINED GLASS. 16TH CENTURY, SOUTH GERMAN. *SCHOOLROOM SCENE.* MANUSCRIPT ILLUMINATION (RIGHT).

# chapter two

WILLIAM H. H. TROOD (1860–1889). *A DOMESTIC SCENE.* OIL ON CANVAS, 1888.

# BREEDS APART

---

Pick a dog, any dog. The range of choice is mind-boggling—from 3-pound Chihuahuas to 220-pound mastiffs, from fleet-footed greyhounds that can sprint at speeds up to 50 miles per hour to low-slung basset hounds that can take 20 minutes to travel a block if you can convince them to make the trip at all, from fluffy fur balls you can carry in your pocket to snarling creatures from hell guaranteed to scare the wits out of anybody. There are dogs bred to be good at retrieving birds shot from the sky, dogs bred to follow vermin into their holes, dogs bred to rescue drowning humans, and dogs bred just because somebody thought they were cute. And there are the mutts, the Heinz-57-varieties dogs, available in an equally wide range of sizes, shapes, and temperaments, bred mainly because nobody stopped them.

The selective breeding of dogs began with our most distant ancestors. Early man fed and bred the dogs he liked and ate the ones he didn't. By the time humans took up writing there were many distinct breeds, some designed to herd animals, others to guard flocks or to fight side by side with their masters. From the beginning there were dogs bred solely for companionship—to be pets.

Our ancestors probably chose a particularly friendly work dog, a hunter or perhaps a herder, and by selective breeding made it smaller—better suited to life indoors. The so-called toys—pocket-size versions of terriers, spaniels, hounds, and just about everything else at one time or another—are the most obvious result of this down-sizing. In the sixteenth century Queen Elizabeth kept a pack of six-inch-tall beagles; unfortunately there is no record of what she used them for. Some of the toys are

THE LABRADOR RETRIEVER, ALSO KNOWN AS THE ST. JOHN'S WATER DOG, WOULD RATHER BE WET THAN NOT.

among the oldest known breeds. The shih tzu, for example, is thought to be descended from ancient Tibetan "holy dogs." Shih tzu means "lion," and these tiny, long-haired favorites of the early Chinese emperors were bred to resemble lions. Other Oriental toy dogs such as the Pekinese and pug supposedly were bred for their flat faces that made them look more like humans than dogs. In the Middle Ages the ladies of the courts of Europe often carried small dogs in their sleeves to protect themselves from fleas; the idea was that the ubiquitous flea preferred dogs to humans. But perhaps the most celebrated toy was a Maltese named Issa, who is said to have charmed even the apostle Paul. Legend has it that Issa, who was the darling of Publius, the Roman governor of Malta, ran away one day and Publius sent out an entire legion to bring her back.

Some breeds were developed to fill well-defined needs. The West Highland white terrier is a case in point. The "Westie" is a short-legged dog related to the Scottish, Skye, Cairn, and Dandie Dinmont terriers. As the story goes, a nineteenth-century Scottish colonel named Edward Donald Malcolm was hunting with a pack of terriers of various colors when he mistook one of his reddish dogs for a fox and shot it. Furious with himself, Malcolm vowed on the spot to breed a pure white terrier so he would never again kill one of his own pack accidentally. The result was the West Highland white. Another Scotch terrier, the Dandie Dinmont, was named after a fictional character who owned six feisty terriers in Sir Walter Scott's historical novel *Guy Mannering*. The novel was a hit, as were the gallant little terriers that Scott described. They are still a popular breed today.

Curiously, some breeds continue to be in favor even after the job they were designed to do no longer exists. Take the enormous Irish wolfhound, still popular despite the fact that there haven't been wolves to hunt in Ireland for more than two hundred years.

The popularity of one breed over another is sometimes hard to understand. In this century the movies have had a lot to do with it. Rin Tin Tin, voted "the most popular star in America" in 1925, started America's continuing love affair with the German shepherd. Lassie did the same for female collies, even though all the dogs who

AMONG ARABS, THE ELEGANT SALUKI, THOUGHT TO BE A GIFT FROM ALLAH, IS ALLOWED TO EAT FROM ITS MASTER'S DISH.

played the role were males. Likewise, poodles have had an extended popular run due in part to their countless film roles and the fact that they come in three convenient sizes: small, medium, and large. Border collies are currently in style, thanks to movies like *Babe*, where one of them adopts a pig. So are Dalmatians, sold in record numbers since the release of Disney's *101 Dalmatians*. Bred as coach dogs on the Dalmatian coast of what used to be Yugoslavia, where they would run alongside teams of coach horses to keep them moving in the right direction, these high-strung, energetic dogs often don't work out as pets, and unfortunately more and more of them are turning up at animal shelters. Movies and television also reflect the popularity of the "macho" dog, what Roger Caras, president of the ASPCA, calls "testosterone on a leash." Says Caras, "You see guys in their late teens to early thirties walking down the street with a chain that could be attached to an aircraft carrier and at the end there's a Rottweiler or pit bull wearing a collar with spikes. They're saying 'fear my dog, fear me.'"

It's too soon to tell if the current First Dog in the White House, Buddy, the Clinton's brown Labrador, will start a run on retrievers or drive them out of favor. It wouldn't be the first time politics influenced the popularity of a breed. In the seventeenth century King Charles II was so fond of a particular variety of spaniel—the small, long-haired, almond-eyed dog with a slightly pointed nose seen in the paintings of Titian, Van Dyck, Gainsborough, and Reynolds—that he gave it the official title of King Charles Spaniel and decreed that the breed be allowed in any public place, even the Houses of Parliament, where until then animals had been strictly forbidden. Charles was a Catholic king and his spaniels were Catholic dogs, the politically correct dogs of the time. His successor, William of Orange, on the other hand, was a Protestant, devoted to a properly Protestant breed, the pug. When William took the throne of England, the King Charles Spaniel instantly fell from favor. More than three centuries later an American named Roswell Eldridge went to Europe in search of Catholic spaniels, particularly those shown in a painting called *The Cavalier's Dogs* by Sir Edwin Landseer. Eldridge couldn't find any, so he set out to recreate the breed on his own. The result was what is now called the Cavalier

King Charles Spaniel, recognized as an official breed by the American Kennel Club (AKC) in 1996.

There are some 55 million dogs in the United States today, living in 35 million households. More people have dogs than have children. About 20 million American dogs are purebreds and some 12 million of them have their bloodlines registered with the AKC; about half the remaining purebreds are registered with organizations such as the United Kennel Club (UKC); the rest are paperless. The AKC divides dogs into seven official groups—Sporting, Hound, Working, Terrier, Non-sporting, Herding, and Toy. There is an additional group known as the Miscellaneous Class, which contains breeds trying to achieve full recognition from the AKC. There are currently four breeds in this class: the Anatolian shepherd, the Havanese, the Lowchen, and the Italian Spinoni. These dogs show in AKC competition but are not eligible for championship points.

Humans have matched their dogs in races and fights and contests of skill and courage for thousands of years, but the notion of a dog show—to see whether my Airedale is better than your Airedale—is fairly recent. The first of what could be considered contemporary dog shows were held in England starting in about 1860. In 1863 a London show judged more than 1,000 dogs, and soon after Americans were conducting similar events. Some critics see the proliferation of dog shows as a side effect of affluence—people with too much time on their hands.

Two million of the 12 million dogs officially recognized as purebreds compete against each other in the hundreds of dog shows sponsored by the AKC each year. Of these, 2,500 make it to the big time: the Westminster Kennel Club all-breed show, the Superbowl of the canine world, held at Madison Square Garden in New York City. Held each February since 1887, Westminster is the second-oldest sporting event in the United States, after the Kentucky Derby. It is a time of black-tie banquets, elaborate awards presentations, and lavish parties where more than dogs are on display. The coveted Best in Show award is the brass ring.

The AKC recognizes 141 of the more than 500 distinct breeds thought to exist in the world today. Some don't exist in the United States in any significant

TOP TO BOTTOM: AMERICAN PIT BULL TERRIER, PUG, DALMATIAN, NORFOLK TERRIER, BULL TERRIER.

THE BERNESE MOUNTAIN DOG
WAS ORIGINALLY USED IN
SWITZERLAND TO GUARD AND
DRIVE CATTLE AND TO PULL
CARTS. BRED TO KILL MICE, RATS,
BADGERS, AND FOXES, THE WELSH
TERRIER (RIGHT) IS SOMETIMES
CALLED "BRITAIN'S FIRST TERRIER."

number and thereby are excluded; others are either not popular enough, not sufficiently documented, or simply out of favor. Interestingly, the only way to tell a purebred from a mixed breed is by its papers. Even the celebrated judges of the Westminster show cannot tell a poodle from a Pomeranian just by looking at it. If you have a dog that looks like a German shepherd and perfectly meets the AKC standard for that breed, you cannot be sure the dog won't sire puppies that resemble spaniels or Chihuahuas unless your dog has papers. A purebred poodle is essentially a dog whose parents looked like poodles, whose grandparents looked like poodles, whose great-grandparents looked like poodles, and so on.

A biologist armed with the latest scientific tools, including sophisticated DNA-testing equipment, cannot even distinguish between dogs, wolves, coyotes, and foxes: All are canines, capable of interbreeding and producing fertile offspring. The ancient Greeks often tied female dogs in heat outside so that wolves could mate with them, and it is said that the Native Americans of the Great Plains bred their dogs with coyotes to make them more intelligent. Even today, dogs and wolves are bred by some kennels to produce exotic guard dogs as well as pets. In fact, as Washington University biologist John Patton put it, "The dog is entirely a man-made artifact."

Quibbling over the meaning of breeds may seem academic, but in recent years it has mushroomed into a political question of some magnitude. Many states have passed or are considering passing breed-specific legislation aimed at outlawing so-called vicious dogs, particularly the pit bull, but also German shepherds, Rottweilers, Doberman pinschers, Akitas, and chow chows. The problem is obvious—how does the enforcement officer distinguish a genuine pit bull from a nasty dog that merely resembles one? The logical—and absurd—conclusion is that only pit bulls registered by the AKC are illegal.

Nevertheless, for most of us the whole question of purebred breeds is unimportant. Our dogs have names like Spot, Spike, or Fluffy rather than Pouch Cove's Make A Wish or Gossamer's Lion of Judah, and they tend to live next to the kitchen stove or under the porch or out in the backyard. It would be interesting to know what they think of such things as stud books and dog shows and distinctions like Best of Breed.

THE TINY ITALIAN GREYHOUND WAS A FAVORITE OF QUEEN VICTORIA AND CATHERINE THE GREAT.

THE POODLE, THE NATIONAL
DOG OF FRANCE, COMES
IN THREE SIZES: TOY,
MINIATURE, AND STANDARD
(SHOWN HERE).

THERE ARE TWO WELSH CORGIS:
THE PEMBROKE (RIGHT) AND
THE CARDIGAN. THE CARDIGAN
HAS A FOXLIKE TAIL, THE
PEMBROKE HARDLY ANY TAIL AT
ALL. CORGI MEANS *DWARF
DOG* IN WELSH.

48

# canine showtime

The hours before a dog show are filled with nervous stomachs, stage fright, and pre-performance jitters—at least for the humans involved. At the Santa Ana Valley Kennel Club show, held in September 1997, the air was charged with tension as the purebreds—both owners and dogs—prepared to go for the proverbial brass ring, Best in Show.

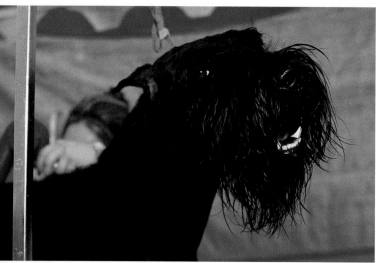

A SNIP HERE, A BRUSH THERE.
LAST MINUTE GROOMING IS
ALL ABOUT LOOKING GOOD
FOR THE JUDGES, AND IN THE
FABULOUS WORLD OF
CANINE COIFFURE THAT CAN
BE VERY GOOD INDEED.

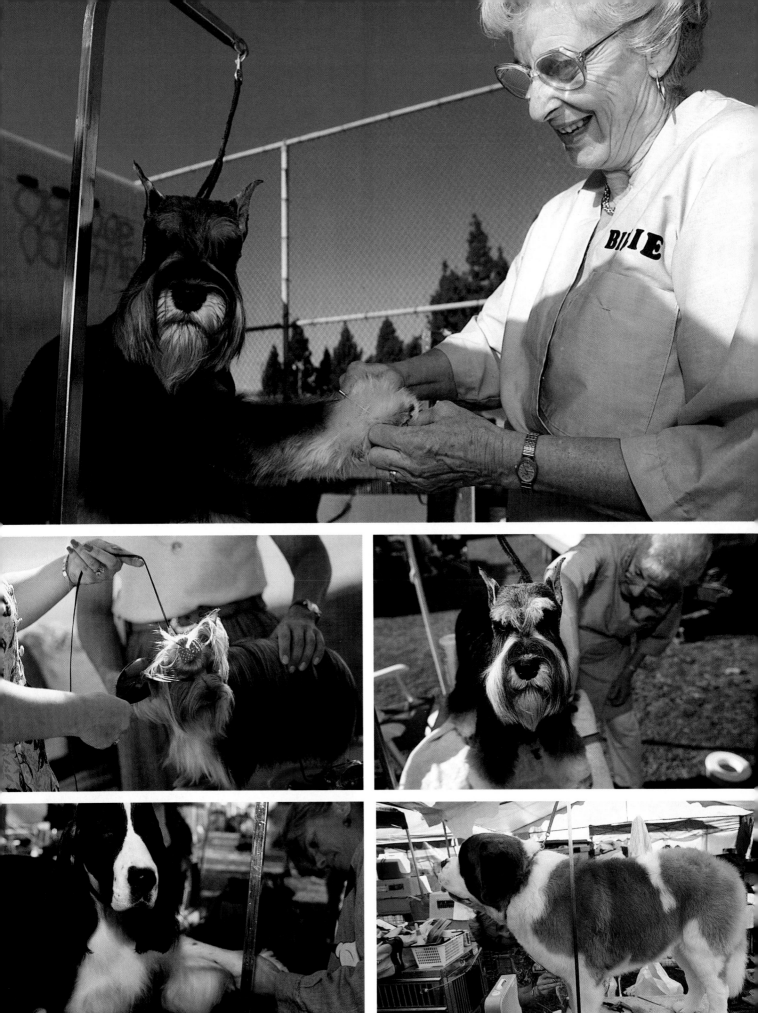

THE JUDGES AT THE SANTA ANA
VALLEY SHOW NOT ONLY
CONSIDERED THE WAY THE DOGS
LOOKED BUT HOW WELL THEY
DISPLAYED SOME OF THE SKILLS
ASSOCIATED WITH THEIR BREEDS.
THE DOGS WERE NOT MEASURED
AGAINST EACH OTHER BUT BY HOW
CLOSELY THEY CONFORMED
TO STANDARDS ESTABLISHED BY
THE AMERICAN KENNEL CLUB.

AT THE END OF THE DAY ONLY ONE DOG TAKES HOME THE CHERISHED BEST IN SHOW RIBBON. ON THIS DAY IN CALIFORNIA IT WAS A WELSH TERRIER NAMED ANASAZI BILLY THE KID.

# a dog is a dog is a dog

Strange as it seems, the elegantly coiffured poodle, the high-spirited Dalmatian, the wrinkled bulldog, and the fleet-footed borzoi are all members of the same species, capable of interbreeding to produce fertile offspring. At first glance, members of a single breed seem carbon copies, but each dog has its own special attitude and personality.

-3-
Appearance
and
Grooming

-2-
Sitting
Politely for
Petting

-1-
Accepting
a Friendly
Stranger

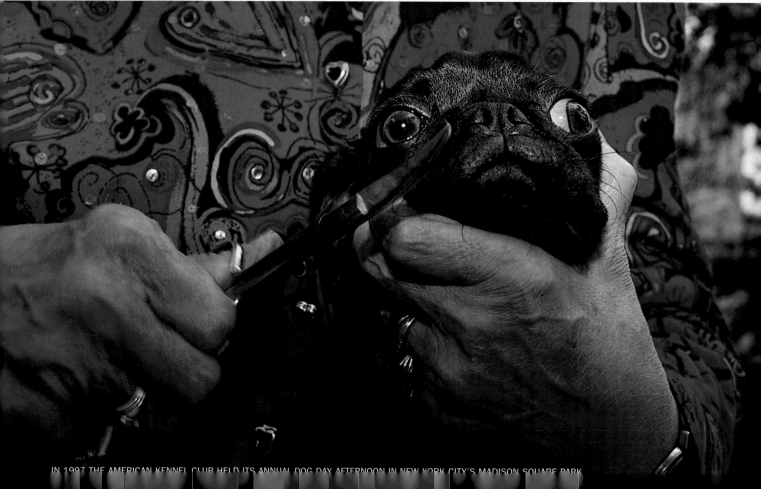

IN 1997 THE AMERICAN KENNEL CLUB HELD ITS ANNUAL DOG DAY AFTERNOON IN NEW YORK CITY'S MADISON SQUARE PARK.

GROOMING, OBEDIENCE TRAINING, CANINE ART, EVEN DANCING DOGS WERE FEATURED AT THIS SEPTEMBER EVENT.

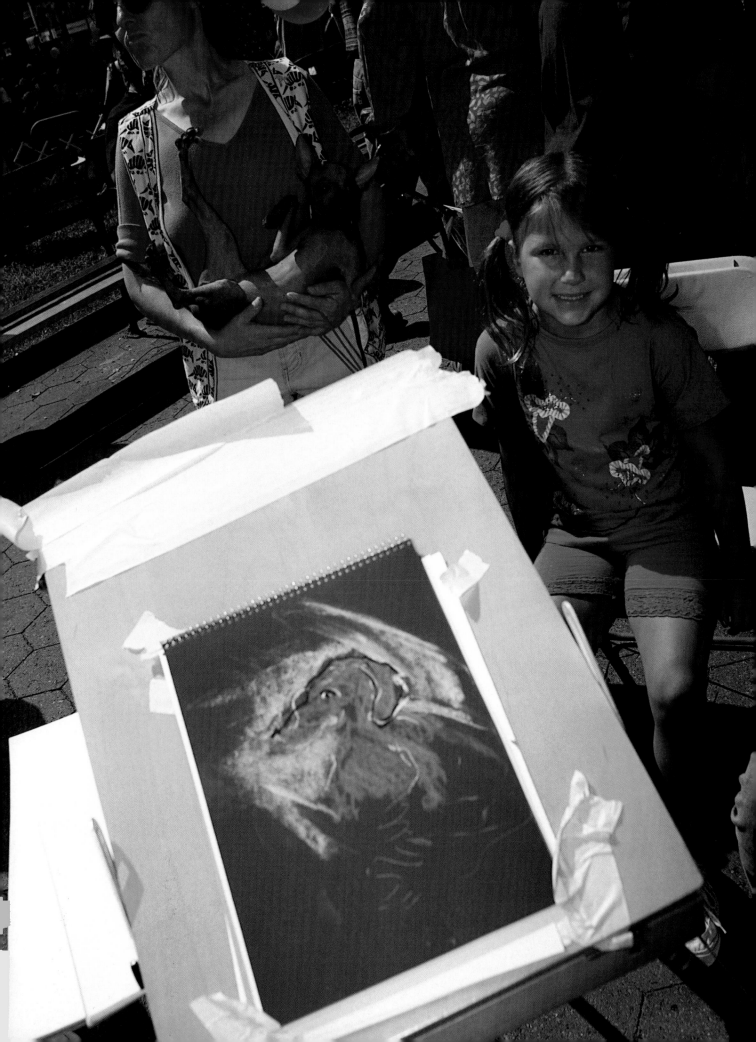

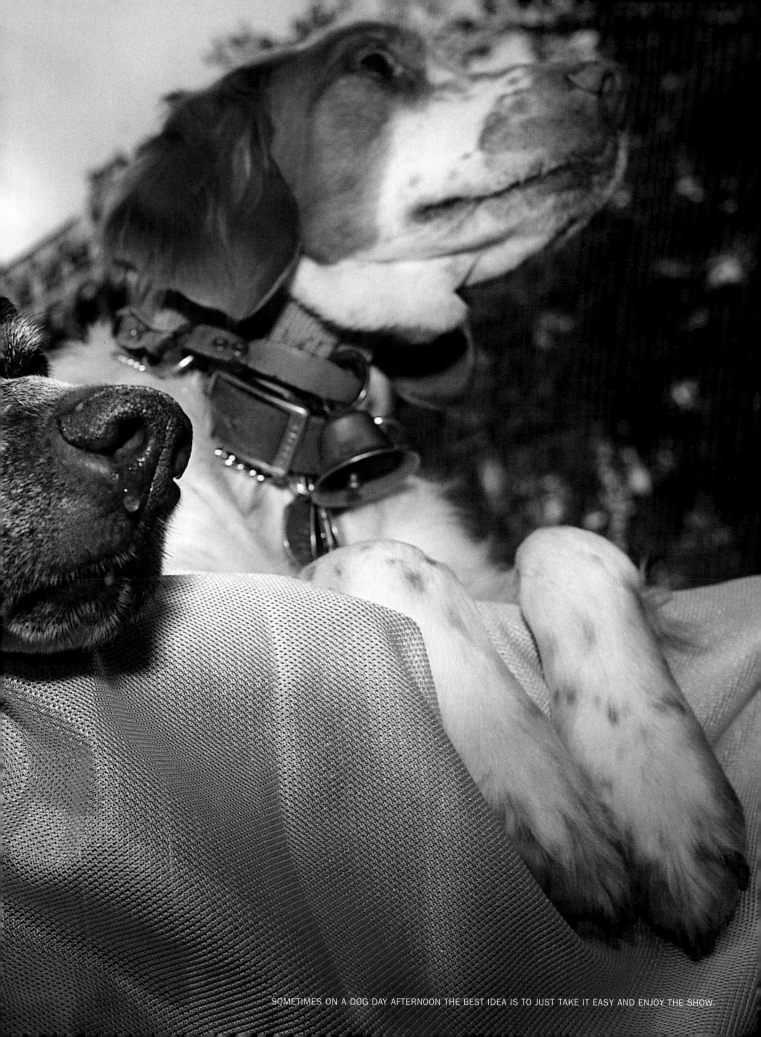

SOMETIMES ON A DOG DAY AFTERNOON THE BEST IDEA IS TO JUST TAKE IT EASY AND ENJOY THE SHOW.

chapter three

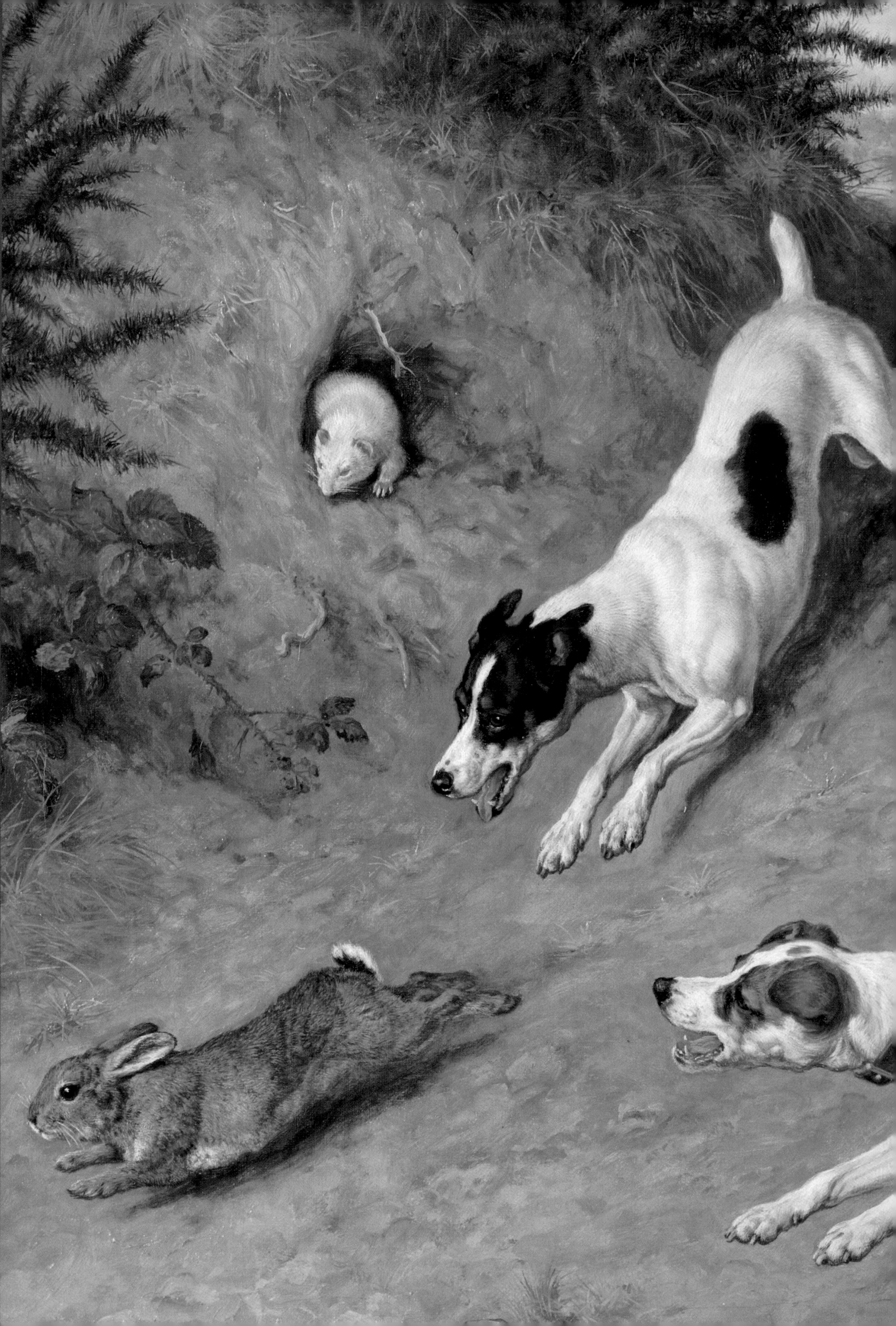

FRANK PATON (1856–1909). *A NEAR MISS.* OIL ON CANVAS, 1892.

# A DOG'S LIFE

One of the reasons dogs and humans get along so well is that neither of us can survive alone. We both evolved from creatures who traveled in packs and required companionship and teamwork to make a life for themselves. "Pack behavior is social behavior," says dog trainer Sapir Weiss. "Dogs want to be part of a group or pack. In order to maintain social order within the pack certain rules of behavior must be observed. Licking, smelling, courting gestures, warning gestures, and correcting are all part of a harmonious dance dogs do with each other and humans too. After all, we are part of their pack; they actually see us as funny-looking dogs."

We in turn often deal with dogs as though they are no more than funny-looking people, perhaps because that's exactly what we wish they were. As TV commentator Andy Rooney put it: "The average dog is a nicer person than the average person." When our dogs are sick we send them not only to doctors (veterinarians) but more and more these days to chiropractors, acupuncturists, and the entire range of holistic practitioners. We feed them organic foods, send them to health clubs and spas, and when they are depressed or agitated we trot them off to psychiatrists, psychologists, therapists of every description—even psychics. And we pamper them as we ourselves wish to be pampered. Consider the services offered at Hollywood Hounds, an exclusive canine salon in Los Angeles. "We have Adrian, the Jose Eber of the grooming and styling world," says owner Susan Marfleet, "and a Rolls Royce available for birthday parties and special events. We also have shiatsu massage, and a Hollywood Hounds clothing line, custom-tailored to you and your dog, and ceremonies

ZERO THE WONDER DOG, WHO PLAYED "PARD" IN THE 1941 FILM CLASSIC *HIGH SIERRA*, SHOWS HIS STUFF.

HOOP NOTWITHSTANDING,
A RELUCTANT BULLDOG
ENDURES THE RIGORS OF
"AGILITY TRAINING" AT A
POSH BEVERLY HILLS
OBEDIENCE SCHOOL.

for people who want to get their dogs married—or Bar Mitzvahed if they're Jewish."

Many veterinarians and dog trainers, however, say the worst thing you can do is treat your dog as though it were a human in a fur suit. Dogs certainly display intelligent behaviors, feelings, and emotions, but they are not human intelligent behaviors, human feelings, or human emotions. "One major misconception," says trainer Shelby Marlow, "is that dogs feel guilt. 'If only I hadn't peed on the floor' and so on. Another is that dogs carry grudges. You know, 'he ate my favorite shoes to get back at me.'"

One way to understand how dogs perceive the world is to compare their sensory tools—eyes, ears, nose, tongue—to those of humans. Humans hear sounds ranging from 20 to 20,000 cycles per second; dogs can detect sounds up to 40,000 cycles per second—thus their well-known ability to hear high-pitched sounds indistinguishable to us. Dogs with erect ears can move them in the direction of sounds, which gives them more acute hearing than their floppy-eared counterparts.

The visual acuity of dogs varies considerably from breed to breed, but the so-called sight hounds—bred to hunt by sight, as opposed to scent hounds—surpass humans

BUSTER, UNDER CONTRACT TO METRO-GOLDWYN-MAYER, CONSIDERS HIS CUE.

in some respects. The field of vision of a good sight hound is almost 270 degrees, whereas a scent hound's may be 180 degrees; by comparison, our own field of vision is only about 120 degrees. Yet dogs have trouble focusing at close range and also exhibit a form of color blindness that alters their perception of reds, greens, and blues. Red appears yellow to them; blues and greens appear white. Dogs' sense of taste also is less developed than in humans, which probably explains why they'll eat almost anything when they're hungry.

Most of all, it is the nose of the dog—as much as a million times more sensitive than the human nose—that truly excels. For this incredible tool we have employed them first in the hunt for game and now in the hunt for everything from drugs to explosives to truffles. The sensory area inside a dog's nose is about 40 times larger than the comparable area inside ours, allowing dogs to perceive and process millions of different smells. They can distinguish between identical twins by scent alone, and some believe they can read our feelings and emotions the same way. They can remember the smells of humans and other dogs they have met in the past. Dogs also appear to possess sensory systems that don't exist in humans, which may allow them to detect earthquakes and even epileptic seizures before they happen. They live in sensory worlds that we humans can only begin to imagine.

As far as we know, dogs don't speak English, or Spanish, or French—at least not in front of us, as Kurt Vonnegut suggested in his short story, "Tom Edison's Shaggy Dog," in which the inventor's dog gives him the secret to the electric light. His fellow dogs soon after tear him to pieces for letting out the fact that dogs can indeed speak.

But do they understand what we say to them? According to veterinarian Michael Fox, author of more than 40 books and a nationally syndicated column on animal medicine: "Dogs are, first of all, acute observers of our body language, and our body language expresses our emotions and intentions. Our tone of voice also expresses our emotional state. Dogs tune into all of this. As for dogs understanding words, a lot of what we say is just blah, blah, blah, whether it's between each other or with our dogs, but there are key words that dogs learn, like 'park' and 'leash' and 'out' and they will cue to them. Intelligent, well-trained dogs have a running vocabulary of forty to sixty words." Fox uses this mixture of verbal and body language with his own dogs. "Our communication is expressed in body language, tone of voice, growls, whines, whimpers," he says. "I can talk in a whining voice or a growling voice. But precise words are important as specific cues. I can say to my dog, 'where are the big birds?' and she immediately looks up for crows; 'Where are squirrels?' and she looks up in the trees. She knows. She has an image of what the word is saying."

While dogs appear to understand human behavior, we frequently are befuddled by theirs. Barking, for example. Why do dogs bark? The latest theory is that dogs bark— all but the basenji, which for some reason doesn't—in part because they are frozen at an adolescent stage of development, the result of our attraction to and breeding of dogs that act like puppies. Their evolutionary ancestor, the wolf, barks as a pup but seldom as an adult. According to biologist Raymond Coppinger and linguist Mark Feinstein at the Cornell College of Veterinary Medicine, dogs bark to sound an alarm, to warn intruders off a marked territory, to express anxiety, to greet their owners and, yes, just for the hell of it. "Therefore," conclude the researchers, "they are loud, obstreperous, repetitious, and a general noisy nuisance, like other adolescents with whom you might be acquainted." The scientists observed all varieties of barking dogs for their study, including a cocker spaniel who managed to squeeze 907 barks into a ten-minute interval.

Jumping up on people is another dog behavior that often confuses humans. Says trainer Shelby Marlow: "Dogs jump up. It's a normal canine greeting. Dogs lick your face. If they're in the wild, they come back and the first thing they do is they lick each other's faces. It's actually quite sweet, although it's often unacceptable in terms of what we're trying to achieve. I use the word 'off,' which means 'don't touch.' I also teach them to sit and I give them a treat for sitting. There are a lot of things you can do in terms of training a dog not to jump up, but you have to know that it's very nice in its origin. It's 'hello, I love you.'"

Tail wagging too may not be all that it seems. It has long been thought that tail wagging was a dog's version of a smile, a sign of pleasure. But whereas humans will smile at a funny picture or a gift from a loved one, researchers now believe that dogs only wag their tails for humans and other dogs, not for inanimate objects. If you bring them food their tails will wag, but if they discover it on their own, with no other humans or dogs present, they will not. Another interesting canine behavior is what trainers call the *play bow*—when a dog lowers its front end by extending its forelegs as though it were praying. As any owner knows, the dog is telling you it's ready to play.

So how smart is your dog? Experts say it depends on the breed and the individual dog. To determine which were the smartest, most easily educated pooches, prizewinning dog trainer and University of British Columbia psychologist Stanley Coren examined records of obedience trials and polled more than 100 top dog judges before coming up with a ranking of 133 breeds, a kind of IQ scale for dogs. At the top of the list was the Border collie, followed by the poodle, German shepherd, golden retriever, and Doberman pinscher. The elegant Afghan, which Coren calls "a perfect fashion accessory," came in dead last. Coren warns, however, that a smart dog is not always the best dog. "Pick a dog on the basis of your lifestyle," he says. "A Border collie is an absolutely terrible dog for a working person. If you have a smart dog you have to spend time with him." As for mutts, Coren says looks are the best indicators of behavior: "If it looks mostly like a German shepherd it will act mostly like a German shepherd."

Of course there are dumb Border collies and poodles, just as somewhere there are probably smart Afghans. There are even stories, as yet undocumented, of basset hounds that will come when you call. Many experts feel it's not the intelligence of the dog that's the problem, but the intelligence of the owner. Says British dog trainer and TV personality Barbara Woodhouse: "I can train any dog in five minutes. It's training the owner that takes longer."

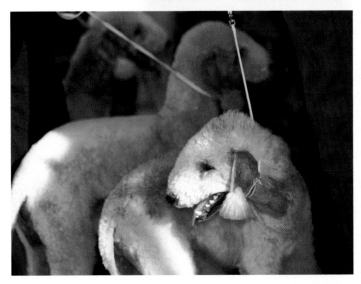

DOGS ARE NOTHING IF NOT CURIOUS. IT MAY HAVE KILLED THE CAT, BUT CURIOSITY FOR A DOG CAN LEAD TO NEW FRIENDS, BURIED TREASURE, AND IF HE GETS LUCKY, MAYBE EVEN A TASTY SANDWICH.

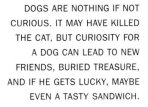

WHETHER IT'S A STICK OR AN OLD SHOE, IF YOU THROW IT YOUR DOG WILL GO AFTER IT AND TRY TO BRING IT BACK. LIKE BEGGING AND OTHER SUBMISSIVE BEHAVIORS, FETCHING IS AN INSTINCT, A LEGACY OF THE ANCIENT PACK.

SHAKE THE PAW OF THE INCOMPARABLE BASSET HOUND, A DOG PRAISED BY SHAKESPEARE AND ELVIS ALIKE.

# high-flying frisbee dogs

It all started in the 1920s when Yale undergraduates started throwing and catching empty pie tins from the Frisbee Pie Company for sport. Wham-O called them Pluto Platters when they released the first plastic discs in 1957, hoping to capitalize on the UFO craze, but changed the name to Frisbee a year later. Dogs probably started catching Frisbees the day they went on sale, snagging the elusive discs far better than humans ever could. Then in the 1970s on national television Alex Stein and his dog Ashley Whippet slipped onto the field during a Dodgers baseball game and put on an incredible—if illegal—demonstration, an aerial ballet of plastic disc and dog. The crowd went wild, and the sport of canine Frisbee was born. Today there are Frisbee dog clubs all over the world devoted to the high-flying antics of these Michael Jordans of the canine world. The clubs hold competitions and award prizes, all leading up to the Super Bowl of canine Frisbee, the Alpo Canine Frisbee Disc World Championships, held in 1997 on the grounds of the Washington Monument. The twenty-third annual championship matched 16 human-dog teams, all leaping for the grand prize of a $1,000 U.S. savings bond and a one-year supply of Alpo. Each dog performed compulsory catch-and-retrieve routines as well as a freestyle program. Frisbee dog competitions also include long-distance events, where the longest throw and catch wins, and accuracy events, where the dogs try to catch the Frisbee within specific marked circles.

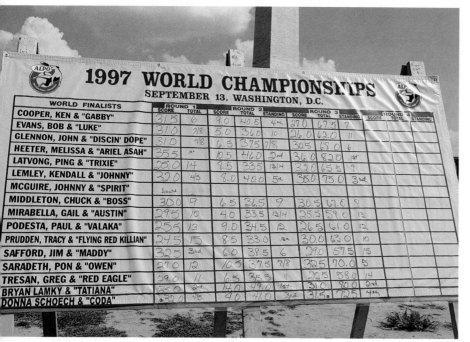

A CANINE CONTENDER PROVES ONCE AND FOR ALL THAT DOGS CAN JUMP.

FRISBEE DOG JUDGING
IS BASED ON SHOWMANSHIP,
LEAPING ABILITY, DEGREE
OF DIFFICULTY, AND
EXECUTION, BUT AT THE
END OF THE DAY EVERY
DOG IS A A WINNER.

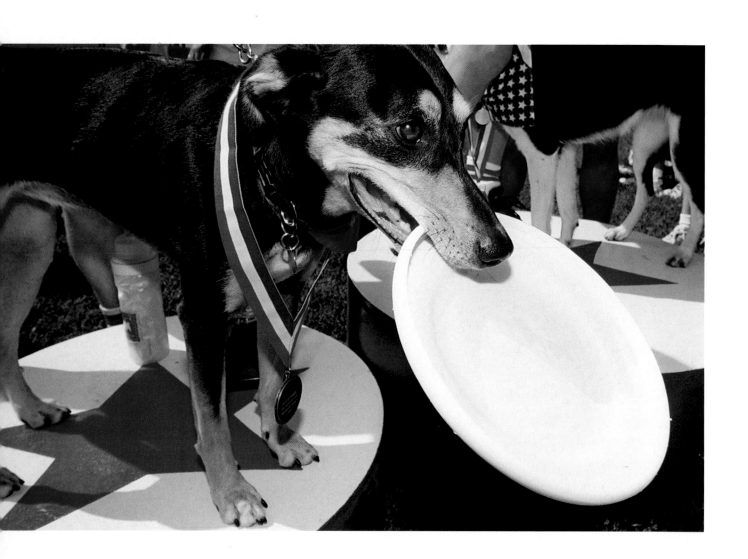

# chapter four

THOMAS BLINKS (1860–1912). *FULL CRY!* OIL ON CANVAS.

# LENDING A PAW

Consider the jobs dogs hold. They guard us and protect our property. They shepherd our sheep, cattle, reindeer—even geese and ducks. Some, such as the Portuguese water dog, at one time herded fish into nets, retrieved lost tackle, and acted as ship-to-ship and ship-to-shore couriers. They pull our carts and sleds and carry our packs. They are unsurpassed at finding everything from lost children to explosives to illegal drugs. They rescue us from treacherous waters, mountain snows, and burning buildings. They assist the elderly and handicapped, guide the blind, detect sounds for the deaf, cheer up the depressed, and still have time for us at the end of a hard day. Many are skilled enough to hold multiple jobs. Says New York congressman Gerald Solomon, chairman of the House Rules Committee: "My dog can bark like a congressman, fetch like an aide, beg like a press secretary, and play dead like a receptionist when the phone rings."

The first working dog was probably a watchdog, hired for alertness and his bark; it's been said that Stone Age man never got a decent night's sleep until he teamed up with the dog. But dogs didn't just settle for warning off possible attacks. When the attacks actually came, some stood their ground, fought, and sometimes died defending the camp; these were the first guard dogs. Before long, watchdogs and guard dogs were employed everywhere. Their function was stated, simply, on an ancient Roman mosaic found in Pompeii—*cave canem*, beware the dog. Psychologist Stanley Coren recently polled trainers who specialize in property and personal protection dogs as well as trainers working with police departments to find out which

VENUS, AN AIR FORCE GUARD DOG, DEMONSTRATES THE FEROCITY OF HER ATTACK.

MINSTREL, RESIDENT CAT OF A BRITISH POLICE DOG SCHOOL, GETS PROPER RESPECT FROM FLEDGLING CANINE COPS.

breeds make the best watchdogs. Among the top 15, as can be expected, are the Rottweiler and German shepherd as well as some surprises, such as the Yorkshire terrier, dachshund, and Chihuahua. As Sir Walter Scott wrote, "Size doesn't matter, just the sound." Coren also came up with a list of breeds "least likely to succeed as watchdogs" that include the Newfoundland, Old English sheepdog, and bloodhound.

Although bloodhounds may not excel at warning people of impending crimes, traditionally they are law enforcement's first choice for tracking down criminals at large and a public icon of police work, as evidenced by the popular cartoon sleuth Inspector Hound and McGruff the Crime Dog, who asks us to "help take a bite outta crime." One of America's most celebrated crimestoppers was a black-and-tan bloodhound named Nick Carter, after the popular detective hero of the "dime novels" of the late nineteenth century. Nick was owned by Lexington, Kentucky, police chief Volney Mullikin, who used him to track down criminals and lost children at the turn of the century. Over his career, Nick was credited with 650 identifications resulting in convictions—one of them by tracking an arsonist over a 105-hour-old trail. (The distance record for tracking, however, is held by a Doberman pinscher named Saur who, according to the *Guinness Book of World Records*, tracked a cattle thief more than 100 miles across the Great Karoo in South Africa in 1925.)

Scent hounds like the bloodhound are known as tracking dogs. They hunt with nose to the ground and require a sample scent, such as that from an article of clothing, to work. But other kinds of dogs are used in rescue work as well, among them what are called air-scenting search dogs. These dogs, such as German shepherds, work with their heads held high, since they smell the air rather than the ground. They do not require scent samples or ground tracks—they can detect the presence of humans over large areas simply by sniffing the air—but they require intensive training and expert handling.

The Saint Bernards bred by Augustinian monks in the mountains between Italy and Switzerland are probably the best-known rescue dogs, although the notion that they carried a small keg of brandy around their necks to revive lost or injured travelers is a myth. There was brandy, but the monks carried it. The Saint Bernards were trained in pairs, male and female, the idea being that when they found a snowbound human, the female would snuggle next to the victim to provide warmth and the male would go for help. These dogs are thought to have saved as many as 2,500 people since they were first bred. The remains of a Saint Bernard named Barry, credited with saving as many as 40 humans over his 14-year life, are preserved in a museum in Bern, Switzerland, as a tribute to that breed. Another celebrated rescue dog, a wire-haired

terrier named Beauty, saved countless human and animal lives from the rubble of war-torn London during the Blitz. After the war Beauty was honored for her gallantry, presented to the queen, and given a citation that allowed her "the freedom of Holland Park and all the trees therein."

Before the invention of firearms dogs were used as weapons of war. One such, the ancestor of today's mastiff, known as the Molossian dog, is thought to have topped 280 pounds and was mean and aggressive as well. Such terrifying canines, armed with spikes or spears or carrying pots of boiling resin, served in many ancient armies and were effective against both foot soldiers and cavalry. Lore has it that Alexander the Great was so fond of a dog named Perites—a dog who allegedly killed a lion in less than a minute and wrestled an elephant to its knees—that he named a conquered city after him. One of Napoleon's troops during the Italian campaign was a poodle named Moustache who received grenadier's rations and rank. Killed by a cannonball, Moustache was given a full military funeral.

DOGS HAVE PERFORMED FOR ASTONISHED AUDIENCES FOR AS LONG AS THERE HAVE BEEN CIRCUSES.

ALMOST EVERY
TURN-OF-THE-CENTURY
FIRE COMPANY HAD A
DOG WHO RACED
ALONGSIDE THE
GALLOPING HORSES ON
THE WAY TO A FIRE.

## THE FIRE DOG

A vanished feature of fire-fighting in New
York. Almost every fire company in the old
days of horse-drawn engines x had its pet dog
who raced to the fire behind the galloping
horses. Some of them followed their masters
into burning buildings and were ready to help
with rescues. This is "Happy", famous xx
25 years ago.

FIRE-DOG "HAPPY."

The unquestioned canine hero of World War II was a mangy mix of shepherd, collie, and husky named Chips, who served in the U.S. Army's K-9 corps in North Africa and Sicily. Chips's duty included guarding Franklin D. Roosevelt and Winston Churchill in Casablanca when they met there in 1943; he was said to have single-pawedly captured a German machine-gun nest, for which he was awarded a Silver Star and Purple Heart. The way the story goes, Chips bolted when George Patton's Seventh Army hit the beaches in Sicily, racing ahead despite repeated calls from his handler. He then leaped into a seemingly abandoned pillbox where seven enemy soldiers were hiding with machine guns. Chips was wounded but still managed to grab one soldier by the neck and, perhaps by sheer valor, caused the six remaining soldiers to surrender without firing a shot. Near the end of the war General Dwight Eisenhower was introduced to Chips who, befitting a fighter loyal to Patton's command, promptly bit the Supreme Allied Commander on the hand.

Throughout history armies employed herding dogs as well, since before the invention of preserved rations and freeze drying armies kept their food on the hoof. The Border collie is the most popular herding dog used today, and it is said that a sheep farmer can replace three hired hands with one good dog. One west Texas goat farmer reports that it took 40 cowboys over a month to round up his goats for shearing before he started using Border collies; now, 10 to15 cowboys and the dogs can do the work in four days. Over the years herding dogs have been bred to fit tasks they are required to perform, as is the case of the Welsh corgi, a short-legged dog designed to slip under the kick of cattle and nip them on the heels to move them in the right direction. But perhaps the most unusual genetic experiment in the world of herding dogs is the English sheepdog, supposedly bred for its lack of a tail—in direct response to an English tax code that placed a levy on any livestock born with a tail.

Hunting dogs too are bred to fit the terrain over which they work. "The three setters are good examples of that," says Dorothy MacDonald, president of the Dog Judges Association. "They all do the same work, but they were designed for different territory. The black-and-tan Gordon setter is a tough dog, bred for the rugged terrain of Scotland. The English setter is softer because it has to run on pretty easy ground.

SHEPHERDS LIKE THIS ONE SERVED VALIANTLY IN VIETNAM.

The Irish setter has to be able to handle the bogs and moors of Ireland." Similarly, hunting dogs were designed for the prey they were meant to hunt, although not always for the prey after which they are named. The Norwegian elkhound, for example, was bred by the Vikings to hunt moose, and the Great Dane was originally a boar-hunting dog. The Rhodesian Ridgeback, a mix of European hounds, dingoes, and wild dogs, was bred to hunt lions and is still said to be the only breed that can keep a lion at bay.

Historically, the dog's keen sense of smell was used primarily for finding game and tracking fugitives. Nowadays, however, the dog's unique ability to detect and identify many different creatures and substances has earned it a variety of new jobs, many of which had been previously handled by machines. In 1997 dogs were used on more than 235 search-and-rescue missions in California alone, sent out to find and assist victims of everything from avalanches to chemical plant explosions. They are even used to find termites in houses. Hawaii employs a team of dogs whose specific job is to screen incoming mail and baggage for snakes—for the state has no snakes and doesn't want any. Lester Kaishi, coordinator of Hawaii's snake inspection team, is especially worried about the brown tree snake, which has wiped out nine species of forest birds on Guam since it was imported to the island after War War II. This snake not only preys on birds but will gladly feast on lizards and even domestic cats. "There's no machine we know of that will do it," says Kaishi. "Dogs are the only known tool that can be used to detect the snake. In this age of electronic technology, man's best friend is still the best friend we have."

There seems to be no limit to the things dogs can do for us. They make us laugh and can give us a kind of comfort we can't get from other people. Some scientists say that just petting a dog can lower your blood pressure and improve your health. They certainly can raise your spirits. You don't even have to own one. In China, in a suburb of Beijing, there is a kennel known as the Divine Land of Beloved Dogs, where people can rent dogs by the hour so they can have the pleasure of walking a dog— without the onus of taking one home.

TRAVIS STOUT AND HIS SERVICE DOG, KOSMIC, WHO HELPS TRAVIS UP WHEN HE FALLS, TAKE EACH OTHER FOR A WALK.

# the beagle brigade

Ever vigilant, the green-jacketed hounds of the Beagle Brigade are America's first line of defense against invasion by harmful agricultural pests and diseases through the nation's ports of entry. At 16 international airports and several U.S. mail facilities, the fine-tuned noses of these beagles sniff passengers, cargo, and mail in search of everything from French liver paté to illegal asparagus from Brazil. In 1995 a dog named Jackpot busted travelers carrying more than a ton of contraband meat products. Recruits at the Brigade's training center in Orlando, Florida, come from shelters, rescue leagues, and private donations, and those that survive the 18-week boot camp typically serve a six-year tour of duty. They work closely with their human partners and often retire to their handlers' homes as pets when their careers with the U.S. Department of Agriculture's Beagle Brigade are over.

THE BEAGLE BRIGADE WAS FOUNDED IN 1984 AND THE FIRST DOGS WORKED AT LOS ANGELES INTERNATIONAL, SNIFFING VISITORS BOUND FOR THE SUMMER OLYMPICS. ORIGINALLY, LARGER DOGS SUCH AS LABRADORS WERE USED, BUT THEY WERE THOUGHT TO INTIMIDATE CROWDS OF PASSENGERS. BEAGLES, BEING SMALL AND PUPPYLIKE EVEN WHEN FULL GROWN AND EQUIPPED WITH A KEEN SENSE OF SMELL, WERE THE PERFECT CHOICE. BLESSED WITH A BOUNDLESS APPETITE, THEY WERE WILLING TO WORK FOR TREATS.

BRIGADE RECRUITS ARE FIRST TRAINED
TO DETECT APPLES. THEY SOON
GRADUATE TO OTHER FOODS AND
EVENTUALLY CAN SNIFF OUT
CONTRABAND WITH GREATER THAN
90 PERCENT ACCURACY.

H erding dogs inherited their skills from wolves who, working in packs, gathered their prey in numbers to a specific location before selecting an individual for the kill. Today there are as many breeds of herding dogs as there are kinds of animals to herd, each designed to match the terrain and livestock they are meant to work. Some herding dogs, among them the popular Border collie, use what breeders and trainers call "eye"—the ability to stare down their charges. These dogs also display what is called "clapping," where they lower themselves close to the ground in a kind of predatory crouch when they face livestock in their care, most likely another useful legacy of ancient wolves.

## keeping them all together

HERDING DOGS COME IN ALL SIZES.
LARGE DOGS SUCH AS GERMAN
SHEPHERDS AND ROTTWEILERS DEFEND
AS WELL AS HERD THEIR FLOCKS.
SMALL DOGS SUCH AS WELSH CORGIES
ARE EXCELLENT HERDERS OF LIVESTOCK
THAT TEND TO KICK, SINCE THEY CAN
SLIP UNDER FLYING HEELS.

EASILY HERDED BY DOGS, DUCKS BEHAVE LIKE SHEEP AND ARE SOMETIMES USED TO TEACH PUPPIES HOW TO WORK.

# chapter five

VICTOR

His

aster's Voice

NIPPER, RCA VICTOR'S TRADEMARK JACK RUSSELL TERRIER, LISTENS FOR HIS MASTER'S VOICE.

# FIDO'S FAME
# & FORTUNE

Every dog has its day. Humans too, according to Andy Warhol, who declared that each of us gets to be famous for 15 minutes. There are several paths to fame and glory if you happen to be a dog. You can attack a famous human, preferably in front of a TV camera, but that kind of fame is fleeting at best. The first thing journalists learn is that Man Bites Dog is a much better story than Dog Bites Man. Probably the best way is to team up with a famous human and bask in your master's limelight. It worked for Odysseus's dog Argus, whose tale has been told for thousands of years. It worked for a black-and-white cocker spaniel named Checkers, immortalized in a speech delivered in 1952 by then vice presidential candidate Richard Milhouse Nixon. The speech was about a now mostly forgotten $18,000 campaign contribution, but it will be forever known as the Checkers speech.

George Washington's dogs—Mopsey, Taster, Cloe, Tipler, Forester, Captain, Lady Rover, Vulcan, Sweetlips, and Searcher, all hounds—received some notoriety during his time as president. So did Abraham Lincoln's dog, Jip. Theodore Roosevelt's dogs— a bull terrier named Pete, a Chesapeake retriever named Sailor Boy, and a mongrel named Skip—had to compete for press coverage with a menagerie of snakes, badgers, roosters, bears, horses, and parrots all living at the White House, not to mention a lion, a hyena, a wildcat, a coyote, a zebra, and a raccoon. Calvin Coolidge kept a dozen dogs during his presidency; Herbert Hoover kept eight. Franklin Delano Roosevelt owned seven dogs during his three terms, the most famous a Scotch terrier named Fala.

EIGHT BLAZE-FACED COLLIES HAVE PLAYED THE PART OF LASSIE SINCE 1943, ALL MALE, ALL OF THE SAME BLOODLINE.

Lyndon Johnson loved beagles despite the names he gave them—Beagle, Little Beagle, Him, and Her—and the winces felt across the country every time he picked one up by the scruff on national TV. Johnson also had a white collie named Blanco and a mongrel named Yuki, his admitted favorite. Yuki and the President liked to howl together. Gerald Ford's White House was home to a golden retriever named Liberty; Jimmy Carter's dog was named Grits. Ronald Reagan kept two dogs at 1600 Pennsylvania Avenue, a Bouvier named Lucky and a King Charles Spaniel named Rex. Then there was Millie, the springer spaniel who wrote a best-selling book while her owner, George Bush, occupied the chair in the Oval Office.

A few dogs have gotten a taste of politics firsthand. Not long ago Al Shugart, president of Seagate, the world's largest manufacturer of computer disk drives, tried

to run his Bernese mountain dog Ernest for Congress in California's Seventeenth Congressional District. The Federal Election Commission wouldn't let Ernest on the ballot but Shugart is challenging the ruling. "Ernest's prime qualification," he says, "is that he has no prior political experience." Legend has it that at least one dog made it all the way to the top. His name was Saur, and supposedly an eleventh-century Norwegian king, angry with his subjects, placed the dog on his throne, where Saur sat and ruled for three years.

Dogs who go where no dogs have gone before often find themselves in the news. One such trailblazer was a Newfoundland named Scannon, who crossed the continent with Lewis and Clark in their famous expedition. Another was a husky mix named Bravo, who made the papers in 1957 when he became the first dog to winter at the South Pole. But the true canine celebrity of the 1950s was a dog named Laika, which is Russian for Barker. On November 3, 1957, Laika, a Moscow stray, boarded a spacecraft called Sputnik II and became the first living creature to orbit the Earth.

Among humans, sports heroes have always enjoyed instant celebrity status. Curiously, the same is not true for dogs. Winners of AKC competitions are virtually unknown outside of the dog show circuit, perhaps because we insist on giving them names like Killiecrankie's Baker St. Mystery (a Gordon setter), Lakshmi Valentino of Jo-Li (a Pekinese), and Sunsprite Absolutely Sable (a miniature pinscher). The incomparable Gary Larson made the point in a *Far Side* cartoon strip titled "The Names We Give Dogs/The Names They Give Themselves." Here Larson presented "Zornorph, the One Who Comes By Night to the Neighbor's Yard," and "Vexorg, Destroyer of Cats and Devourer of Chickens," and the unforgettable "Princess Sheewana, Barker of Great Annoyance and Daughter of Queen La, Stainer of Persian Rugs."

The literature of famous dogs begins with Dick and Jane and their dog, Spot. "See Spot run" is one of the first complete sentences many of us learned to read. Today's kids, in turn, learn of the world from such canine mentors as Sergeant Murphy, the police officer dog of Richard Scarry's *What Do People Do All Day?* Then there is Buck, the sled-dog hero of Jack London's *Call of the Wild;* Cabal (sometimes spelled

FRANKLIN D. ROOSEVELT WITH HIS SCOTCH TERRIER FALA (LEFT).

Caval), King Arthur's dog in Tennyson's *Idylls of the King;* Lad, the collie hero of Albert Payson Terhune's *Lad, a Dog;* and a real-life, black unclipped poodle named Charley, memorialized in John Steinbeck's *Travels with Charley*. Of course all fictional dogs are not heroes, as evidenced by Arthur Conan Doyle's terrifying *Hound of the Baskervilles* and Stephen King's *Cujo*. There are even a few fictional dogs with drinking problems, most notably Neil, the martini-guzzling ghost Saint Bernard of Thorne Smith's novels *Topper* (1926) and *Topper Takes a Trip* (1932), later made into three movies and a TV series.

The era of the dog as Hollywood star began in 1924, when a German shepherd named Rin Tin Tin captured the hearts of silent-movie audiences everywhere. Called Rinty by his trainers, the first canine movie star was allegedly found in an abandoned German trench during World War I by an American named Lee Duncan, who brought him to Los Angeles after the war and trained him for the movies. Rin Tin Tin himself made more than 40 movies, and after his death in 1932 the role was played first by his son, Junior, and later by a series of lookalikes. But the all-time canine star of movies and television, the dog who earned top billing over the likes of Elizabeth Taylor and James Stewart, was a blaze-faced collie named Pal, star of the 1943 smash hit *Lassie Come Home*. One reviewer of the first Lassie movie described the captivating collie as "Greer Garson in furs."

The world instantly fell in love with Lassie and a string of sequels followed, in addition to a long-running radio show and finally the popular TV series. Bob Weatherax, owner and trainer of the current Lassie, tells how it all started: "My father was training dogs in those days and this guy brought him this collie that chased motorcycles. His name was Pal and at first my father couldn't break him either. Finally, the owner said, 'Look, I don't want the dog back. It's nicer around my house without him.' My father took the dog in lieu of a fee the man owed him. Actually, Lassie was purchased for ten dollars." Weatherax's father had already trained the dog who played Asta in the celebrated *Thin Man* series with William Powell and Myrna Loy, as well as the dog who played Daisy in the *Dagwood* movies with Penny Singleton and Arthur Lake. So when he heard the casting call for *Lassie Come Home*

VICE PRESIDENTIAL CANDIDATE RICHARD NIXON WITH CHECKERS IN 1952.

he took Pal, even though the part called for a female and Pal was male. "He knew what he was doing," says Bob Weatherax. "It took about six months in those days to do a movie and female collies lose their coats twice as fast as males. So with a female it looks like you have a different dog at the end. Besides, you can't tell the sex of a collie because of the long hair." In the end Pal got the part, despite his gender. All the subsequent Lassies were Pal's direct descendants, and all were male.

The popularity of various breeds in the entertainment media rises and falls for reasons unknown. Basset hounds became popular with Cleo, whose thoughts you could hear on TV's *The People's Choice*. There were several memorable bassets named Fred, among them little Ricky's puppy on *I Love Lucy*, truck-driving Jerry Reed's sidekick in *Smokey and the Bandit*, and the low-slung Fred Basset of comic strip fame. Today Jack Russell terriers are the rage, most notably Eddie, one of the stars of the NBC sitcom *Frasier*. Eddie (whose real name is Moose) also parachuted into Super Bowl '96 with *Seinfeld* star Jason Alexander and was featured in the Kentucky Fried Chicken's Super Bowl '97 commercial. Other Jack Russell terriers have appeared prominently in such films as *Clean Slate*, *Ernest Goes to Jail*, *Crimson Tide*, and *The Mask*. Wishbone, the star of his own PBS children's series, is a Jack Russell, as is Hagis, the star of Nissan's "Dogs Love Trucks!" commercials, and the renowned RCA signature dog, Nipper.

Dogs have been portrayed in every manner imaginable, from Harvey, the young hero's dog in Steven Spielberg's *E.T.* to Spuds McKenzie, "America's Favorite Party Animal," according to Budweiser. There was Rags, Woody Allen's robot dog in *Sleeper*, and Matisse, the neurotic Border collie in *Down & Out in Beverly Hills*. And there was Blood, the telepathic sidekick of a young Don Johnson in Harlan Ellison's searing satire *A Boy and His Dog*, in which a beautiful woman and a dog try to prove who is really Man's best friend. The most famous cartoon dog is undoubtedly Snoopy, Charlie Brown's remarkable beagle. There are smart cartoon dogs, such as Brain, Penny's crime-solving dog on *Inspector Gadget*, and Mr. Peabody, who's always instructing his young friend Sherman on *The Adventures of Rocky & Bullwinkle*—and there are not-so-smart dogs, like Disney's Goofy, and the always depressed Droopy.

LYNDON JOHNSON AND FAMILY WITH BEAGLES HIM AND HER.

There's Rowlf, the piano-playing Muppet dog whose favorite composer is Poochini, and there's even a cat named Bowser, who got canine billing in the *Mr. Magoo* cartoons (since the nearsighted hero thought he was a dog).

Some people are concerned that the real show-biz dogs—the canine actors in film and television—are overworked, even abused, by their trainers and owners. "Not true at all," says veteran trainer Captain Haggerty, who trained the first dog to play Sandy in the Broadway musical *Annie*. "They have a great life and the reason is they're working. They enjoy it. They have a job. If you have a problem with a dog the best thing to do is to give him a job. These animals have a great life, much better than your household pet, believe me. And they get the best food and the best medical care, whatever they need. If I had to be reincarnated I'd like to come back as a show-business dog. Or a stud dog."

So every dog has its day, its 15 minutes of fame. Of course it's human fame. For dogs, the true marks of love and glory are the ones they leave on lamp posts and fire hydrants.

OUR GANG'S PETE THE PUP WITH SPANKY MCFARLAND (FAR LEFT) AND THE REST OF THE LITTLE RASCALS.

A WIRE-HAIR TERRIER NAMED
ASTA CO-STARRED WITH WILLIAM
POWELL AND MYRNA LOY
(AS HUSBAND-AND-WIFE
DETECTIVES NICK AND NORA
CHARLES) IN THE *THIN MAN*
MOVIES OF THE 1930S AND '40S.
JUDY GARLAND (AS DOROTHY)
SHARED THE SCREEN WITH A
CAIRN TERRIER NAMED TOTO IN
*THE WIZARD OF OZ*.

CANINE STARS LIKE WONDER
DOG RIN TIN TIN (TOP LEFT),
TOPPER'S MARTINI-GUZZLING
SAINT BERNARD, NEIL (LEFT),
AND THE GANG FROM DISNEY'S
*LADY AND THE TRAMP* ALL
CAPTIVATED AMERICAN
MOVIE AUDIENCES.

LITTLE ORPHAN ANNIE'S DOG SANDY (LEFT) AND EDDIE, THE JACK RUSSELL TERRIER CO-STAR OF THE HIT SITCOM *FRASIER*.

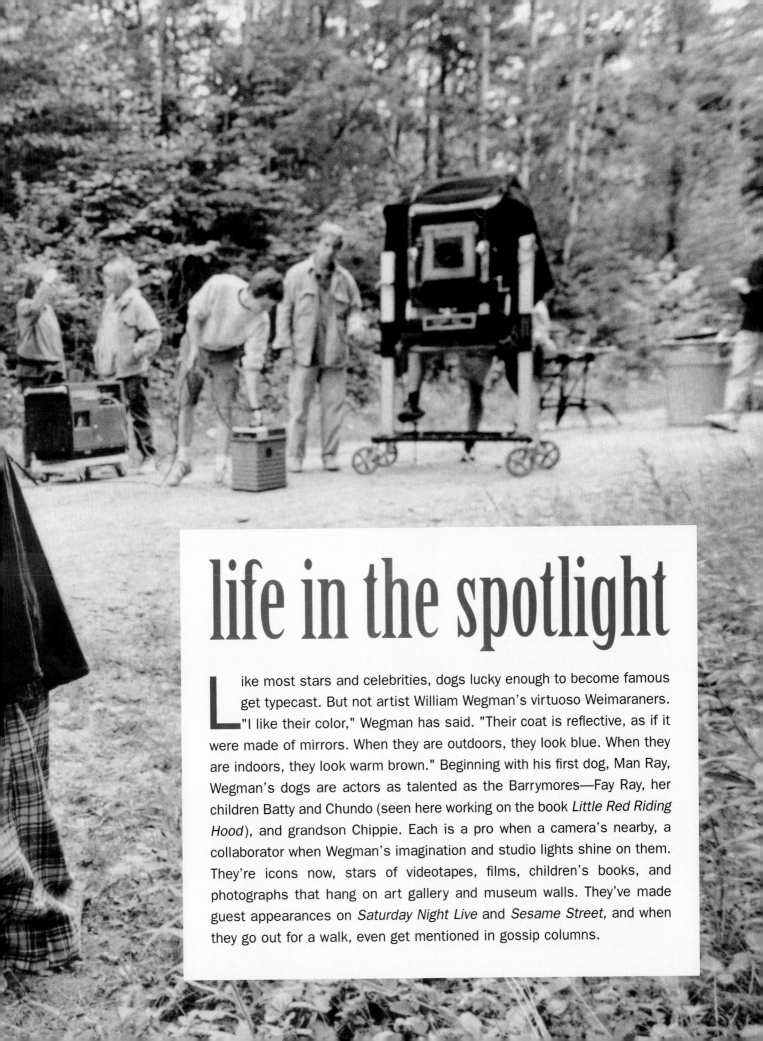

# life in the spotlight

Like most stars and celebrities, dogs lucky enough to become famous get typecast. But not artist William Wegman's virtuoso Weimaraners. "I like their color," Wegman has said. "Their coat is reflective, as if it were made of mirrors. When they are outdoors, they look blue. When they are indoors, they look warm brown." Beginning with his first dog, Man Ray, Wegman's dogs are actors as talented as the Barrymores—Fay Ray, her children Batty and Chundo (seen here working on the book *Little Red Riding Hood*), and grandson Chippie. Each is a pro when a camera's nearby, a collaborator when Wegman's imagination and studio lights shine on them. They're icons now, stars of videotapes, films, children's books, and photographs that hang on art gallery and museum walls. They've made guest appearances on *Saturday Night Live* and *Sesame Street,* and when they go out for a walk, even get mentioned in gossip columns.

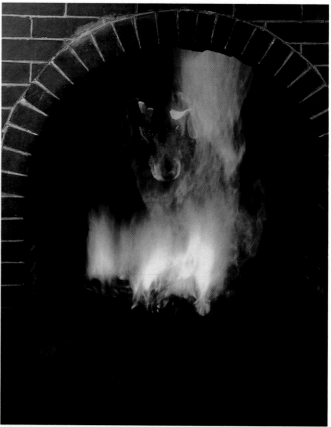

*COUNTRY ROAD*, 1990 (TOP LEFT); *BAD DOG*, 1981 (TOP RIGHT); *RAY AND MRS. LUBNER IN BED WATCHING TV*, 1981 (BOTTOM LEFT); *ELEPHANT*, 1979 (BOTTOM RIGHT).

# a star's best friend

They say it's lonely at the top, so it's no wonder countless stars of movies and television have turned to dogs for companionship. When Oprah Winfrey was asked by a Federal judge to describe herself, she responded, "I have a talk show. I'm single. I have eight dogs— five golden retrievers, two black Labs, and a mongrel. I have four years of college." In the cutthroat world of show business, the unquestioning loyalty of a dog must seem a gift from the gods. Says actor Lee Marvin, "If your home burns down, rescue the dogs. At least they'll be faithful to you."

A FRIEND OF JOAN CRAWFORD AWAITS HER RETURN. LUCY AND DESI WITH THEIR DOGS (RIGHT).

EDDIE FISHER, DEBBIE REYNOLDS, AND FRIEND. DIRECTOR ALFRED HITCHCOCK AT WORK (RIGHT).

BOB HOPE WITH HIS FAVORITE STRAIGHT MAN (LEFT). CLINT EASTWOOD WITH MEMBERS OF HIS PACK.

# chapter six

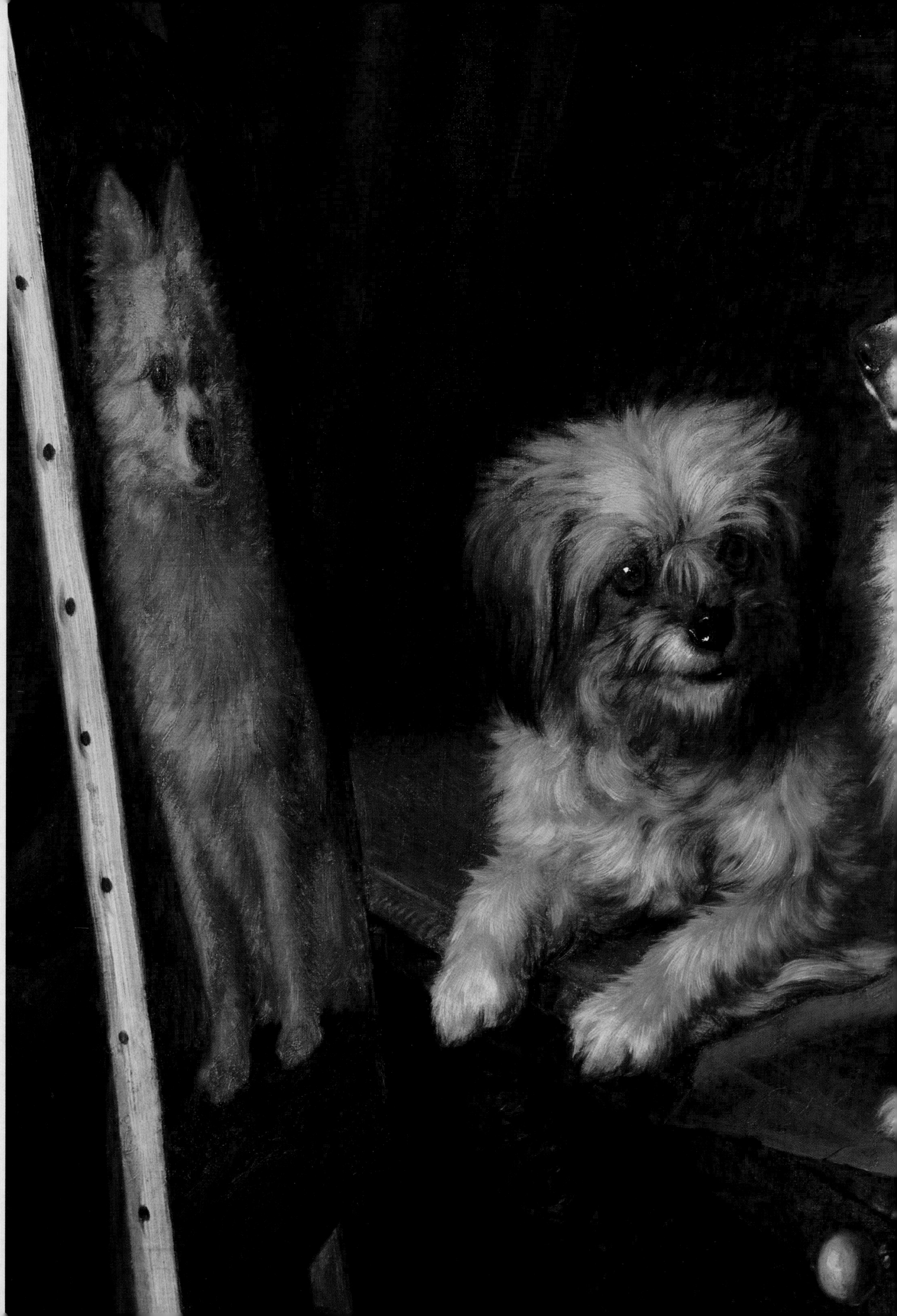

HORATIO HENRY COULDERY (1832–1893). *A TRUE REFLECTION.* OIL ON CANVAS, 1870.

# MUTTS, MONEY,

Here are the numbers: About 55 million dogs and 60 million cats live in the United States and the Humane Society estimates another 70,000 are born each day—seven for every human born. Approximately 35 million households have dogs, more than 30 million have cats, 10 million have tropical fish, 6 million have birds, and another 5 million house pets ranging from aardvarks to zooplankton. All in all we spend about $32 billion on them each year, more than half of it going to the dogs.

According to the American Pet Products Manufacturers Association, almost 60 percent of American pet owners live in metropolitan areas with populations of more than 500,000, and almost half have household incomes over $40,000 per year. More than half of the dogs purchased in 1997 were purebreds. According to the AKC, the most popular breed by far was the Labrador retriever with 149,505 registrations, followed, respectively, by Rottweilers (89,687), German shepherds (79,076), golden retrievers (68,993), beagles (59,946), poodles (56,803), dachshunds (48,425), cocker spaniels (45,305), Yorkshire terriers (40,216), and Pomeranians (39,712). The high rollers appear to be New York City dog owners, who spend $720 million annually on their canine companions, followed closely by dog people in Chicago ($684 million), Los Angeles ($676 million), Washington ($449 million), Philadelphia ($442 million), and Detroit ($370 million).

Writing in the *Washington Times*, reporter Dawn Kopecki recently profiled some of the pampered pooches living around the nation's capital, among them Lucky, a 14-year-old, 32-pound Japanese spitz owned by Mame Reiley, former chief of staff to

# AND MADNESS

ONE OF 400 WORLDWIDE, THE PETSMART IN PHOENIX SELLS MORE THAN 12,000 ITEMS AND RUNS ITS OWN PET HOSPITAL.

Virginia congressman James P. Moran. Lucky has her coat groomed every week at a salon called Pretty Pets and has her own private nanny, at a cost to her owner of nearly $250 per month. Reiley estimates she spends about $5,000 per year on Lucky but is glad to do it: "She's my best friend and confidante. She's like a child." Colleen Evans's two Jack Russell terriers, Jack and Jane, get their monthly makeovers at Chichie's Canine Design and Grooming Spa in Georgetown, where Bob and Elizabeth Dole's schnauzer, Leader, comes for the water- and aromatherapy treatment. When they're traveling, Evans and her husband board Jack and Jane at Shady Spring Boarding Kennel and Camp for Dogs—what she calls "yuppy puppy camp"—at a cost of more than $60 per day for the two dogs. As for dog food, one of the terriers has allergies, so Mrs. Evans prepares a special recipe of sautéed ground turkey with brown rice, vegetables, garlic, and soy sauce, as prescribed by her homeopathic veterinarian.

"The dog industry is growing more than 20 percent a year," says Susan Marfleet, owner of Hollywood Hounds, a posh Los Angeles salon that's been called "a Planet Hollywood for dogs." According to Marfleet: "One of the reasons this is happening is because we live alone—don't necessarily get married and have children by the time we're thirty. And dogs give you unconditional love and they are very cuddly and compassionate to boot. So what a great idea. You know? Get a dog, especially if you're not in a relationship and don't have children. It's the best companion you could have." Hollywood Hounds, which has a statue of Rocky and Bullwinkle outside its Sunset Strip location, also sells a line of canine couture. "We have custom leather jackets," says Marfleet. "We have tuxedos. We have bridal wear. We have reversible rain gear with a Dalmatian print on one side and faux fur on the other. We've got baseball hats and Breakfast at Tiffany's hats—you name it, we've got it."

Although dog pampering seems to be enjoying a recent surge in popularity, it isn't anything new.

"Renaissance canines fortunate enough to live with doting aristocrats often enjoyed the same opulent fashions as their masters," writes anthropologist Mary Elizabeth Thurston in her fascinating *Lost History of the Canine Race*. "Tended to by professional groomers called 'demoiselles,' curly-coated retrieving breeds (thought to be progenitors of the modern poodle) invited creative embellishment in the hands of itinerant canine stylists." Thurston tells of demoiselles who worked along the banks of the Seine under the Pont-des-Arts in nineteenth-century Paris, washing dogs, dipping them in sulfur water to kill the fleas, and clipping them in the most fashionable cuts. "It was during this time," writes Thurston, "that canine coiffures were increasingly patterned after women's hairstyles. The 'tonte en macarons,' a cascade of coiled hair first worn by Princess Eugenie, wife of Emperor Napoleon III, became the rage of the 1890s, inspiring the 'caniche corde,' or corded poodle."

Thurston traces the evolution of canine grooming from the "page-boy bobs" worn by both women and dogs in the Roaring Twenties to the long, natural cuts that characterized both in the freewheeling sixties, when for the first time in history mutts came into fashion. What's next? "On the advent of the twenty-first century," says Thurston, "canine fashion has overcome its image as a snobbish excess to be reborn as a legitimate means of expressing concern and affection for companion animals."

A large part of the $18 billion spent on dogs annually goes toward their health care, not only in traditional veterinarian fees but also on what might be called alternative medicine for dogs. At The Total Dog in Westwood, California, for example, your pooch can be treated with chiropractic therapy, swim therapy, and even acupuncture. Says Total Dog founder Annie Wald: "Acupuncture is a procedure that is basically even better for dogs than it can be for humans. They respond better. They do not walk

IT'S HARD TO FIND A DOG WITHOUT A MAGAZINE DEDICATED TO IT, WHETHER IT'S *THE BICHON FRISE REPORTER* OR *THE POODLE REVIEW*. AND IF READING ABOUT YOUR PREFERRED POOCH ISN'T ENOUGH, YOU CAN FIND SOMEONE WHO WILL CAPTURE YOUR FAVORITE DOG'S LIKENESS ON A STATUE OR PERHAPS A COFFEE CUP.

in with a preconceived idea or notion that they're going to have needles put in their bodies. The procedure alleviates pain from spinal problems and helps arthritic conditions." And more and more traditional vets are now offering ancillary services such as grooming, boarding, training, and the sale of pet products in order to compete in today's dog-eat-dog world. Veterinarian Gordon Davis has turned his McLean, Virginia, office with a staff of 11 veterinarians into a one-stop animal care center to finance the expensive equipment he requires to conduct a modern veterinary practice. Says Davis: "Vets today are investing millions of dollars in their facilities so they can provide state-of-the-art medicine. . . . If it weren't for the ancillary services, I could not afford this high-quality facility."

So why do we do it? Why do we spend so much money on four-legged creatures who can't talk? A recent survey of more than 1,000 pet owners conducted by the American Animal Hospital Association provides some clues. Perhaps the most surprising finding was that 57 percent of the owners surveyed wanted their pet as their only companion if they were shipwrecked on a deserted island. Nearly 80 percent admitted to buying their pets holiday or birthday presents, 33 percent claimed they talked to their pets on the phone or through their answering machines, 21 percent said they sometimes dressed up their pets, 62 percent signed letters and cards from themselves and their pets, and 55 percent considered their pets to be their children. A remarkable 6 percent of dog owners, according to Brideline (an internet web site devoted to matrimonial affairs), include their dogs in their wedding or honeymoon. "How does one appropriately include one's dog in one's wedding?" asked the site's editors. "Mutt of Honor," was one suggestion: "Don't worry if Fido looks silly in the dress, he'll never wear it again anyway." They also recommend the Bouquet Fetch: "It's a long-standing wedding tradition, but with a twist. Bachelorettes are required to snag the bouquet from a 'beg' position, and in their teeth. The winner not only becomes next-in-line for the altar, but gets a snack and a scratch behind the ears."

That's the good news. The bad news is that there are too many unwanted pets, so many that some 12 million are euthanized in shelters each year. More than 61

CONE-SHAPED COLLARS KEEP FIDO FROM GNAWING SORES AND STITCHES, AND FROM STEALING FOOD OFF THE GROUND.

percent of the dogs that enter a shelter are eventually killed, and up to 75 percent of the cats. It costs about $100 to capture, house, feed, and eventually kill a stray animal, for a total of about $1.2 billion per year, most of it from the nation's taxpayers. Some critics think the shelter system itself is partly to blame. Despite the fact that shelters are operated by caring, compassionate people, they do our killing for us, behind closed doors, and so make it easier for people to abandon their pets. Robert Heinlein's novel *Time Enough for Love,* the story of the world's oldest man, Lazarus Long, contains the notebook entries of this fictional Methuselah, words of wisdom for his descendants. One particularly revealing entry reads: "When the need arises, and it does, you must be able to shoot your own dog. Don't farm it out. That doesn't make it nicer, it makes it worse."

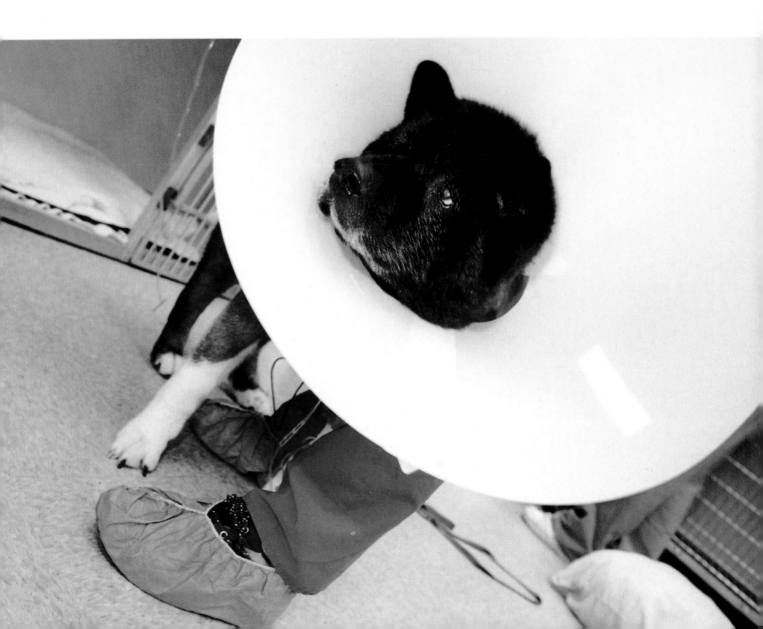

AFTER BACK SURGERY, SWIMMING IS GOOD THERAPY FOR BOTH HUMANS AND DOGS.

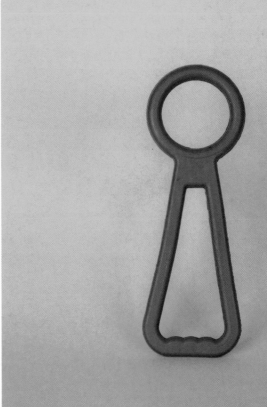

DOGS, LIKE HUMANS,
LOVE TOYS, ESPECIALLY
IF THEY CAN CHEW
THEM AND CHASE THEM
AND, AFTER A WHILE,
GROW TO LOVE THEM.

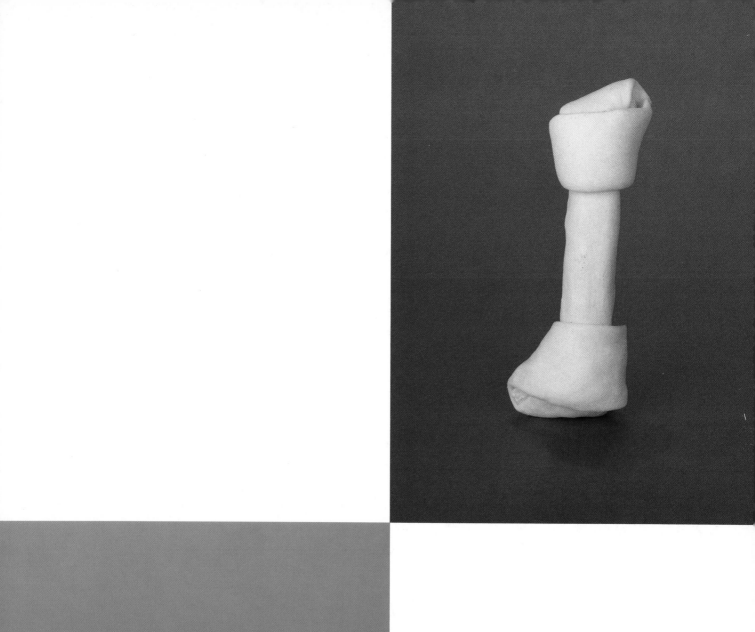

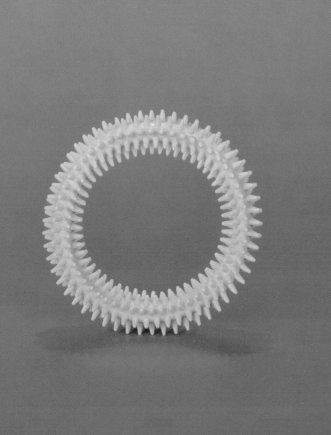

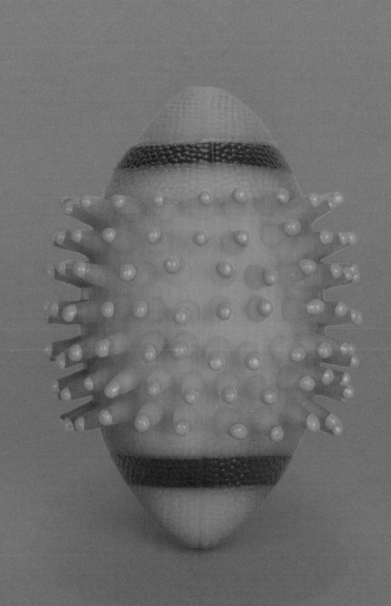

FIDO'S RETREAT AT L.A.'S POSH HOLLYWOOD HOUNDS, A ROOM DEDICATED TO WATCHING VIDEOS AND TAKING NAPS.

A BIRTHDAY PARTY AT HOLLYWOOD HOUNDS CAN COST AN OWNER FROM $200 TO $2,000.

**OZZIE**
10·5·90 — 10·16·91

WE MISS YOU
OZZIE PUPPERINO
ONLY THE GREAT DIE YOUNG
FOREVER IN OUR HEARTS

STEVE & NAN

**SATAN**
1971 ——— 1982

OUR LIVES ARE RICHER
BECAUSE YOU ALLOWED
US TO SHARE YOURS

MANDALL
**MIKKO**
1·22·83 – 4·19·94
MOST PRECIOUS PUPPY
**HEATHER**
9·3·90 – 6·2·95
MOST BELOVED BABY

EACH ONE A SP
JOY AND TREA
WHO WILL LAST
OUR HEARTS
MINDS FOREV

WEISKOPF
**TIFFANY**
1981 — 1992
WE LOVE YOU
**TAWNY**
1978 — 1992

**PATCHES**
JUST WANTED LOVE
FEB. 1991 — DEC. 1993

TORRINGTON

IPPY
U FOR
S SO
& LOVE

**MINN**
OUR FIRST
DEC. 1960 – D

**WIENER SCHNITZEL**
1974 ——— 1990

REST IN PEACE SWEET
BELOVED LITTLE WIENIE
OUR PRECIOUS BABY BOY
FOREVER TO BE LOVED
FOREVER TO BE MISSED
ALWAYS IN OUR HEARTS
LOVE,
MOMMY AND DADDY

BAKER

C·QQ·104

DUKE
197

FOREVER I
AND ALWAYS
MEMORIES O
SUNSHINE

BILL AN

BJ

OUR BE
OLIV
1972 —

SCHIND

MY PAL
MR. UGLY
JAN. 28, 1987

# chapter seven

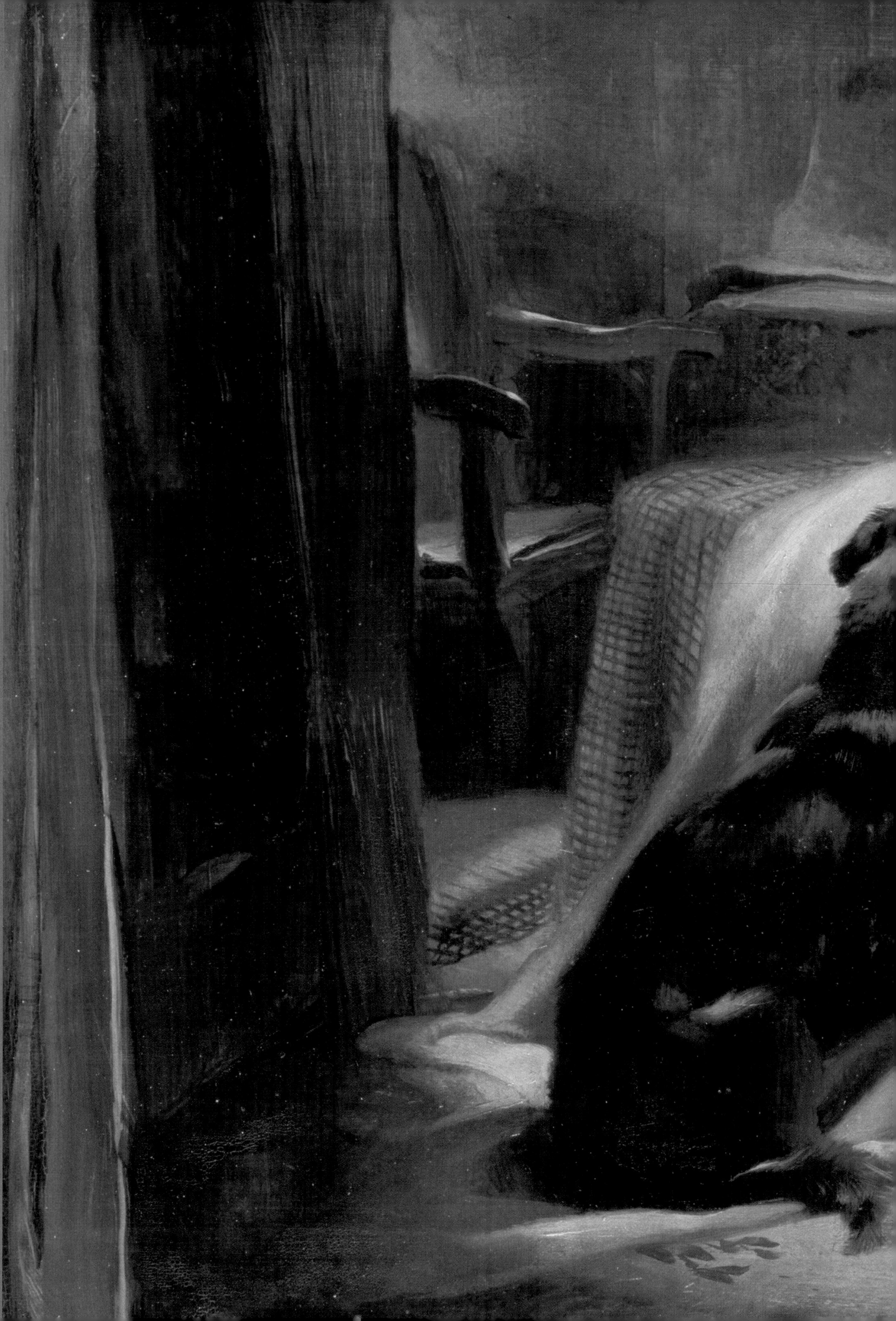

SIR EDWIN HENRY LANDSEER (1802–1873). *THE OLD SHEPHERD'S CHIEF MOURNER*. OIL ON CANVAS.

# THE DEAL WITH DOGS

It often seems that dogs got the short end of the bargain that day long ago, when they first struck a deal with humans. Mark Twain said it: "Heaven goes by favor. If it went by merit, you would stay out and your dog would go in." If you need proof, look no further than the assistance dogs, those highly skilled, expertly trained professionals who team up with disabled humans—one on one, for life—in a partnership that at times defies description.

There are three kinds of assistance dogs: guide dogs, hearing ear dogs, and service dogs. Guide dogs assist the blind and visually impaired, and are sometimes called Seeing Eye dogs or Pilot dogs, although such distinctions only apply to dogs trained by specific kennels, in the same way the term *Xerox* applies only to copies from that specific brand of photocopier. In turn, hearing ear dogs assist deaf or hearing-impaired humans by alerting them to such aural signals as doorbells, telephones, oncoming vehicles, alarm clocks, and smoke alarms. Many of the smaller breeds make excellent hearing ear dogs. Service dogs are trained to help people afflicted with a physical disability other than blindness or deafness, among them those who require wheelchairs or crutches and people with a wide variety of other medical disorders. Service dogs are trained to retrieve necessary items, open doors, find help in an emergency, even call 911. Some, known as seizure alert dogs, can detect epileptic fits before their human charges realize the seizures are coming and are trained to respond appropriately.

"We believe that the seizure alert dogs are picking up on a scent that's created by electrical and chemical changes in the body prior to the clinical signs of the seizure actually occurring," says Darlene Sullivan, executive director of Canine Partners for

Life, a nonprofit organization in Cochranville, Pennsylvania, that trains service dogs and their human partners. "We have no scientific proof, but we know the successful seizure alert dog is usually a very intense dog, very scent focused with a high activity level. They are very intelligent dogs, sometimes a little too smart for their own good. They're the dogs that never sleep. They close their eyes, but if the wind changes, one eye pops open. They're the dogs that have already figured out how to communicate with people. They'll bring you their bowl if they're hungry. They'll bring you their leash if they want to go for a walk. They've already figured out how to make people listen to them."

It was Canine Partners for Life who matched Bob Levasek, who suffers from muscular dystrophy, with his service dog, Joe. "First, they came and interviewed me in my home," says Levasek, describing how his relationship with Joe began. "They were trying to find out what I needed Joe to do—you know, carry things, pick things up, get the phone when it was ringing, that sort of thing. He spent the next six months being custom-trained for exactly what I needed him to do for me. Then we spent three weeks together in team training. In the same way you get a new car and need to learn where the turn signals and the headlight buttons are, I needed to learn the commands Joe had been taught so I could operate him in a safe manner. Joe was smarter than I was at the beginning. He knew what he needed to do and how to do it. It was just me figuring out the right words in the right tone of voice, and just the sound of my voice was enough for him to perform. In the last two and a half years, I've spent more time with Joe than with anybody else I've ever known. He knows my particular nuances, my moods, my frustrations, and my happiness. He's my best friend."

Assistance dogs and other service animals are allowed by law to enter any building or public place in the country when they are on the job. According to the Americans with Disabilities Act: "Service Animal means any guide dog, signal dog, or other animal individually trained to do work or perform

THE EMOTIONAL BOND BETWEEN CANINE AND HUMAN CAN BEGIN WITH A WET LICK ON THE FACE.

tasks for the benefit of an individual with a disability, including but not limited to guiding individuals with impaired vision, alerting individuals with impaired hearing to intruders, providing minimal rescue or protection work, pulling a wheelchair or fetching dropped items." As such, assistance dogs differ from so-called therapy dogs, who need little training—"It's important to not train the brains out of a therapy dog," says one expert—and who require permission to enter establishments such as hospitals or nursing homes and are governed by state and local laws.

Therapy dogs work by just being dogs, bringing joy and often improved health to sick children, the elderly, and the emotionally distraught. A recent UCLA study confirmed that elderly people who own pets make fewer doctor visits than those who live without them. "The benefits of therapy dogs are enormous," says Madeline Bernstein, president of SPCA LA, a group that takes these caring canines to hospitals, nursing homes, and children's clinics in the Los Angeles area. "We've seen people who have not spoken a word to anyone in years suddenly start talking to a therapy dog. And you know, the strangest things happen with these dogs. My own dog, for example, won't sit when you tell him to. If you throw a ball he just looks at you like you must be kidding. Yet when he goes into the Shriner's Hospital to visit children, he sits when I say sit, lies down when I say lie down. When the children call him by name, even if it's not his own name, he comes. All of a sudden I have this championship trained dog who, minutes after we leave the hospital, starts ignoring me again."

The ability of dogs to reduce stress and bring joy to the seriously depressed raises an interesting question: Why not make them welcome in that most stressful of locations, the workplace? In fact, many Americans already do just that. At Autodesk, a computer software company in San Rafael, California, about 100 of the 800 employees bring their dogs to work every day. The dogs sleep under desks, play on the lawns, and get treats from a cookie jar kept at the front desk. There are rules, of course: no barking, no fighting, and three poops on the floor and you're out. The arrangement has worked both for workers and management. The employees—even those who don't own dogs—seem to benefit from the presence of their canine

SOME PEOPLE CARRY PICTURES OF THEIR DOGS IN THEIR WALLETS; OTHERS WEAR THEM ON THEIR SHIRTS.

co-workers. Management discovered that before instituting the bring-your-dog-to-work policy their employees were leaving early because they had to get home to feed and walk their pets. Now, with their dogs beside them, they tend to stay late, increasing productivity.

In the early 1970s an 80-pound, brown-and-white basset hound named Bosley showed up every day for work in the San Francisco offices of the *Saturday Review,* at that time a publisher of four magazines. He attended high-level editorial meetings where, it was rumored, he was involved in selecting which stories made it into print and which did not. The offices were housed in a four-story converted ice house and Bosley had the run of the place. Water bowls were set out for him on every floor but being a true dog, Bosley preferred drinking out of the toilets in the bathrooms. When he wanted to change floors, he stood in front of the elevator until someone came to help him. At first, an employee would ring for the self-service elevator, ride with the dog to another floor, and then return to his or her desk; after a while, though, staff members would simply reach inside the elevator, push a button, and let Bosley take it from there. Visitors frequently were startled, then amused, when the elevator doors would open on the first-floor reception area and an enormous basset hound would amble out, looking like he owned the place. When the publisher went bankrupt in 1973, Bosley made the newspapers as far away as New York City.

All over America are monuments to dogs that have touched our lives. In New York City's Central Park a bronze statue commemorates the exploits of an Alaskan Malamute named Balto, memorialized as Balto the Wonder Dog on many of Johnny Carson's late-night monologues. During a deadly diphtheria epidemic in 1925 Balto led a sled carrying life-giving serum on the final leg of its trek from Anchorage to Nome after his master went snow blind. In the National Postal Museum in Washington, D.C., the stuffed remains of a mutt named Owney honor the memory of a dog who, in the late nineteenth century, accompanied mailmen on more than 140,000 miles of their appointed rounds. The unofficial mascot of the U.S. Postal Service, Owney was said to love anyone who smelled like a mailbag. In Fort Benton,

176

Montana, a bronze statue of a collie named Shep recalls the devotion and loyalty of a dog who, for six years after his owner's dead body was shipped back East on the Great Northern Railroad, met every westbound train in hopes that his master would return. And in Makanda, Illinois, a stone monument commemorates a remarkable three-legged dog named Boomer. The plaque on the monument reads: "In memory of Boomer the hound dog. Tradition says he dashed his life out against the iron abutment of the railroad bridge 300 feet south of this point on September 2, 1859, while running along on three legs trying to put out the flame in a hotbox on the speeding train of his beloved fireman-master."

Dogs play such an important role in our lives and play it so well that sometimes it appears they exist on a higher moral and ethical plane than mere mortal humans. In short, they often seem better than us, superior to us. James Thurber said it: "If I have any belief about immortality, it is that certain dogs I have known will go to heaven, and very, very few persons." All over the Internet are ever-expanding lists of reasons why dogs are better than men, women, or children, depending on your persuasion. Here's a sampling: Dogs are better than men because dogs can be housebroken, they don't have hangups about expressing affection, they don't make fun of the way you run or throw a baseball, and not one of them voted to confirm Clarence Thomas. Dogs are better than women because they never want you to ask for directions, they find you amusing when you're drunk, and they will forgive you for playing with other dogs. As for their superiority to kids, dogs don't bring their messy friends home, don't tie up the phone, and don't like heavy metal or experiment with drugs.

The deal between humans and dogs has survived and flourished throughout the ages in large part because dogs wag their tails and not their tongues. Moreover, they listen to us—at times so attentively that it seems merely the sound of our words must be magically spellbinding. "No one," said Christopher Morley, "appreciates the very special genius of your conversation as a dog does."

The deal with dogs? It's the best deal we ever made.

# special girl special dog

Emily Ramsey has epileptic seizures. Her dog, Watson, always close by, somehow knows when a seizure is about to occur, even before Emily does. When he detects an upcoming event, Watson alerts Emily, who in turn alerts an adult, usually her mom or dad or a teacher at school. Then she lies down, Watson at her side, and waits out the seizure. Emily has taught Watson to open doors and fetch things for her, but her self-appointed guardian angel also makes decisions on his own. He will not permit her to climb stairs if he thinks she is unstable, and will wrap himself around her if he thinks she's losing her balance, giving her not two but six legs for support. Watson can prejudge the severity of a seizure, and even though he seems to detect even the smallest events, he will only alert Emily to those that are likely to endanger her. A regular dog when he's not on the job, Watson doesn't like being away from Emily for any reason. One of a growing number of seizure alert dogs working in the United States, Watson was paired with Emily by Canine Partners for Life, a Pennsylvania organization that trains service dogs.

BIKE RIDING WAS SOMETHING
EMILY COULDN'T DO BEFORE SHE
TEAMED UP WITH WATSON.

WATSON WAS AN ABANDONED
DOG ABOUT TO BE PUT TO
SLEEP WHEN HE WAS RESCUED
BY A VOLUNTEER FROM
CANINE PARTNERS FOR LIFE.
THEN ALONG CAME EMILY AND
WATSON'S CAREER AS A YOUNG
GIRL'S GUARDIAN AND BEST
FRIEND BEGAN.

WATSON STICKS CLOSE TO EMILY EVEN WHEN SHE GOES FOR A SWIM.

In December 1983 New York photography dealer Janet Borden left the ASPCA with a three-month-old puppy, part black Lab, part schnauzer. Standing on the street corner, Borden tested out some names. "Dora?" she asked. No response. "Lucy?" No response. "Clara?" The puppy perked up, picking out her own name. Over the years, Clara went everywhere: to school, to work, even to the library. She loved the smell of the ocean, yellow tennis balls, cat food, car rides, Halloween trick-or-treating, and shopping at Macy's. As her human family expanded—first new dad Chris, then brother Fred—Clara accepted and protected each new member. She was a smart dog and got noticed. Clara was written about and photographed for *The New York Times* and mentioned in *The New Yorker.* She died in 1997, having lived a very full and charmed dog's life.

# PICTURE CREDITS

AMERICAN KENNEL CLUB MUSEUM OF THE DOG: 34–35; ANIMALS ANIMALS: 11, 12, 15, 19, 80, 81, 82–83; ARCHIVE PHOTOS: 99, 143, 144, 145, 146, 147; ART RESOURCE: 16–17 (GIRAUDON), 26–27 (ERICH LESSING), 28–29 (ERICH LESSING), 30–31 (ERICH LESSING), 32 (VICTORIA & ALBERT MUSEUM, LONDON), 33 (SCALA), 92–93 (FINE ART PHOTOGRAPHIC LIBRARY, LONDON), 168–169 (VICTORIA & ALBERT MUSEUM, LONDON); TOM BAMBERGER: 178–179, 180, 181, 182–183; JANET BORDEN: 185, 192; DAVID BUTOW: 2–3, 4–5, 6, 13, 70, 71, 72–73, 155, 156–157, 186-187, 191; EDUARDO CITRINBLUM: 162–163, 164–165; CORBIS-BETTMANN: 78, 95, 96–97, 103, 105, 124, 126–127, 129; CULVER PICTURES: 24, 69, 74, 100–101, 120–121; MADELEINE DE SINETY: 138–139; LAUREN GREENFIELD: 50, 51, 52, 53, 54, 55, 56, 57, 79 (TOP LEFT, BOTTOM LEFT), 152, 153, 172 (BOTTOM); MARVIN HEIFERMAN: 166, 167; JEFF JACOBSON: 114–115, 116, 117, 118–119; JAY MALLIN: 84, 85, 86, 87, 88, 89, 90, 91; JEFF MERMELSTEIN: 60, 61, 62, 63, 64–65, 79 (TOP RIGHT, CENTER LEFT, BOTTOM RIGHT), 171, 172 (TOP FOUR), 174–175, 189; PETSMART: 151; PHOTOFEST: 123, 130–131, 132, 133, 134, 135, 136, 137, 142; FRANCESCA RICHER: 25; RICHARD ROSS: 21, 22, 58–59; WILLIAM SECORD GALLERY INC.: 66–67, 148–149; VALERIE SHAFF: 37, 38, 42, 43, 44, 46–47, 48–49; BEN VAN HOOK: 106–107, 108, 109, 110–111, 112–113; WILLIAM WEGMAN: 140, 141 (ALL COURTESY OF PACEWILDENSTEINMACGILL GALLERY, NEW YORK); NEIL WINOKUR: 41, 158, 159, 160, 161, 184.

# ACKNOWLEDGMENTS

WE'RE ESPECIALLY GRATEFUL TO LESLIE STOKER, EDITORIAL DIRECTOR OF GT PUBLISHING, WHO BROUGHT THIS PROJECT TO US AND WHO HAS BEEN A JOY TO WORK WITH. THANKS AS WELL TO MIMI O'CONNOR AND JIM FREY AT GT, WHO'VE MADE THIS PROCESS GO SMOOTHLY AND PROFESSIONALLY. AT THE A&E NETWORK, WE APPRECIATE THE SUPPORT OF JONATHAN PAISNER, WHO MADE THIS PROJECT POSSIBLE. IN THE EARLY STAGES OF THE BOOK PROCESS, WE WORKED CLOSELY WITH NANCY GIMBRONE, SUE NADELL, DEBBIE SUPNIK, AND JOHANNA LACK AT WELLER GROSSMAN PRODUCTIONS IN BURBANK, CALIFORNIA. WE'D ALSO LIKE TO THANK MICHAEL WILDE FOR HIS THOUGHTFUL COPYEDITING.

THE INFORMATION IN *BIG DOGS LITTLE DOGS,* AS WELL AS ITS SENSE OF FUN AND ENERGY, IS COMMUNICATED LARGELY THROUGH PICTURES, AND FOR THOSE WE THANK THE PHOTOGRAPHERS AND ARTISTS WHO PARTICIPATED IN THE PROJECT: TOM BAMBERGER, DAVID BUTOW, EDDIE CITRINBLUM, KENT AND DONNA DANNEN, MADELEINE DE SINETY, LAUREN GREENFIELD, JEFF JACOBSON, JAY MALLIN, JEFF MERMELSTEIN, RICHARD ROSS, VALERIE SHAFF, BEN VAN HOOK, WILLIAM WEGMAN, AND NEIL WINOKUR. WITHOUT THE HELP OF KEVIN KWAN, WE NEVER COULD HAVE KEPT TRACK OF THE PICTURES COMING IN AND OUT THE DOOR.

TO OUR FRIENDS AND COLLEAGUES AT ART GALLERIES, PICTURE AGENCIES, PHOTO ARCHIVES, AND SPECIAL COLLECTIONS, THANKS FOR THE ADVICE, HELP, AND COOPERATION: BARBARA JEDDA, AMERICAN KENNEL CLUB MUSEUM OF THE DOG; MICHAEL SHULMAN, ARCHIVE PHOTOS, NEW YORK; DIANA REEVE, ART RESOURCE; EVE KLOEPPER, ANIMALS ANIMALS; JOCELYN CLAPP, CORBIS-BETTMANN; ALLEN REUBEN, CULVER PICTURES; KENT AND DONNA DANNEN; SARA STREDNEY, PETSMART; RON AND HOWARD MANDELBAUM, PHOTOFEST, NEW YORK; WILLIAM SECORD; AND BRIDGET SHIELDS AND MARIE WARSH AT THE WILLIAM WEGMAN STUDIO.

SPECIAL THANKS TO MAURICE BERGER, JANET BORDEN, BILL HUNT, FRED MARSHALL, SPENCER MONK, STEPHEN ROMANO AT RICCO/MARESCA GALLERY, CHRIS SHIPLEY, FRED SHIPLEY, JASON WALZ, AND PETER WILLIAMS.

"IF A DOG WILL NOT COME TO YOU AFTER
HAVING LOOKED YOU IN THE FACE,
YOU SHOULD GO HOME AND EXAMINE YOUR CONSCIENCE."
—WOODROW WILSON

190

BIG DOGS LITTLE DOGS WAS PACKAGED BY LOOKOUT BOOKS, NEW YORK.

PRODUCERS: MARVIN HEIFERMAN AND CAROLE KISMARIC

DESIGNER: FRANCESCA RICHER

WRITER: FRANK KENDIG

PROJECT EDITOR: AKIKO TAKANO

PROJECT MANAGER: LINDA FERRER AND THE PICTURE EDITING GROUP

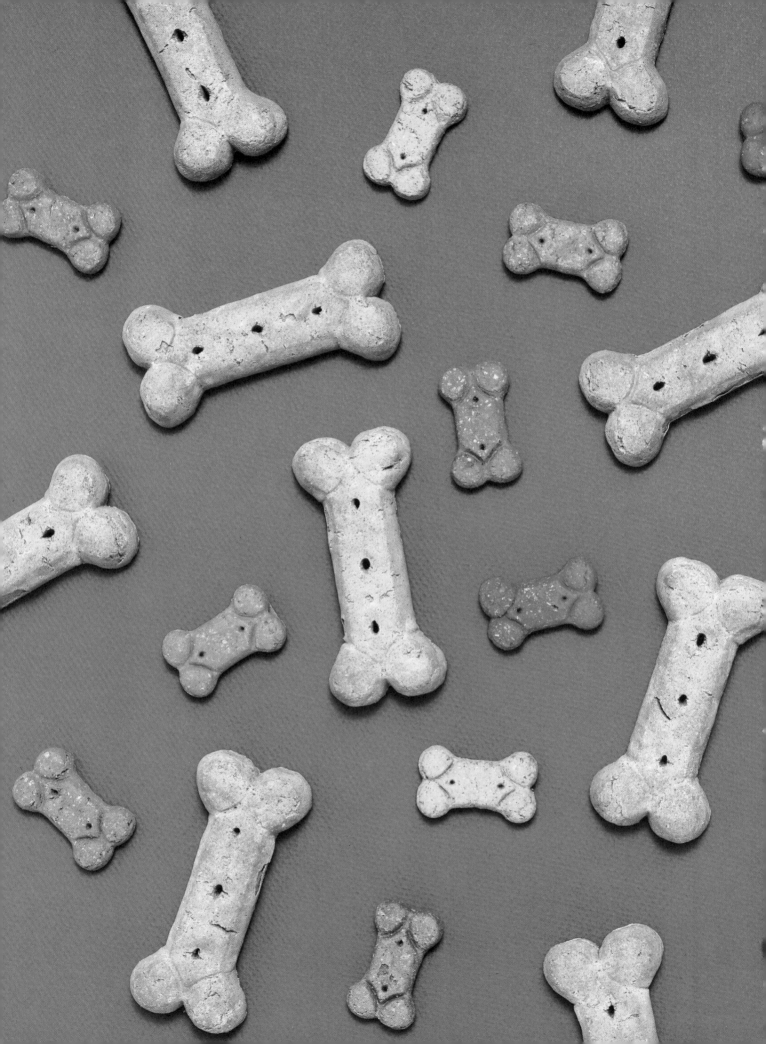